DORLING KINDERSLEY 📖 EYEWITNESS BOOKS

CASTLE

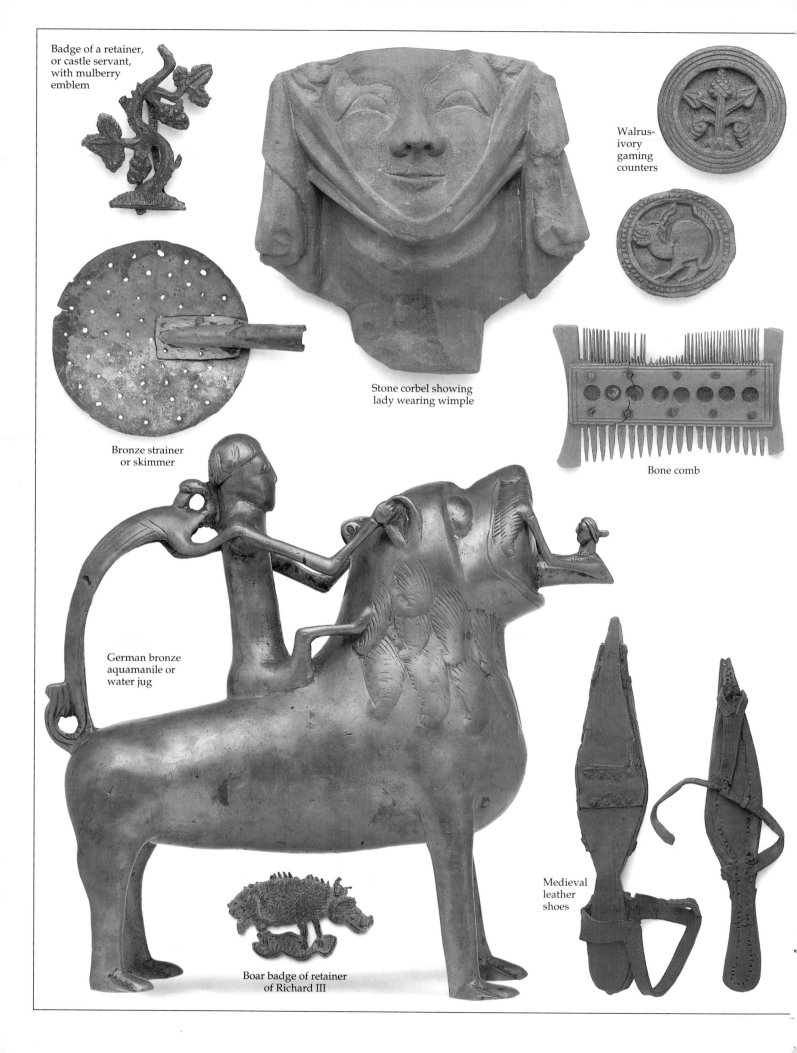

Badge of a retainer, or castle servant, with mulberry emblem

Walrus-ivory gaming counters

Bronze strainer or skimmer

Stone corbel showing lady wearing wimple

Bone comb

German bronze aquamanile or water jug

Boar badge of retainer of Richard III

Medieval leather shoes

Medieval
musician playing
hornpipe

DK EYEWITNESS BOOKS

CASTLE

Medieval peasant
dressed for work in
the fields

Written by
CHRISTOPHER GRAVETT

Photographed by
GEOFF DANN

Ceramic tiles from Tring, England

English pendant
belonging to
castle retainer

Dorling Kindersley

Italian silver
medallion with arms
of Cresci family

15th-century silver-gilt spoon

Walrus-ivory
counter
showing
burial scene

Late 14th-
century
table knife

Stone figure
of St. George

DK

Dorling Kindersley

LONDON, NEW YORK, AUCKLAND, DELHI, JOHANNESBURG, MUNICH, PARIS and SYDNEY

For a full catalog, visit

DK www.dk.com

Project editor Phil Wilkinson
Art editor Jane Tetzlaff
Managing editor Simon Adams
Managing art editor Julia Harris
Research Céline Carez
Picture research Kathy Lockley
Production Catherine Semark
Additional Photography Torla Evans
of the Museum of London, Janet Murray of the British Museum,
Geoff Brightling, Alan Hills, Tim Ridley, and Dave Rudkin

This Eyewitness ® Book has been conceived by
Dorling Kindersley Limited and Editions Gallimard

© 1994 Dorling Kindersley Limited
This edition © 2000 Dorling Kindersley Limited
First American edition, 1994

Published in the United States by
Dorling Kindersley Publishing, Inc.
375 Hudson Street,
New York, NY 10014
4 6 8 10 9 7 5

Dorling Kindersley books are available at special discounts for
bulk purchases for sales promotions or premiums. Special
editions, including personalized covers, excerpts of existing
guides, and corporate imprints can be created in large
quantities for specific needs. For more information, contact Special
Markets Dept., Dorling Kindersley Publishing, Inc.

Library of Congress Cataloging-in-Publication Data
Gravett, Christopher.
Castle / written by Christopher Gravett.
p. cm.—(Eyewitness Books)
Includes index.
1. Fortification—Europe—History—Juvenile literature.
2. Castles—Europe—History—Juvenile literature.
[1. Castles. 2. Fortification.] I. Title.
UG428.G734 2000
623'.14'0902—dc20   93-32594
ISBN 0-7894-5889-6 (pb)
ISBN 0-7894-5888-8 (hc)

Color reproduction by Colourscan, Singapore
Printed in China by Toppan Printing Co. (Shenzhen) Ltd.

Early 14th-
century silver-
gilt belt mount

12th-century
candlestick
from
northern
Germany

Earthenware
ram's-head jug

Contents

Flemish 15th-century covered
wooden bowl (or mazer)

What is a castle?

MANY OF THE GREAT fortifications of the Middle Ages are standing today, still dominating the surrounding countryside. Why were they originally built and who lived in them? A castle was the fortified private residence of a lord. The lord could be a king or a lesser baron, but in either case the castle was a home as well as a stronghold. A castle was designed to be safe against the cavalry charge of knights, so safe that it could withstand a lengthy assault or siege by an enemy. A castle was also a community with many staff: the constable or castellan looked after the buildings and defenses; the marshal was in charge of the horses, garrison, and outside servants; the chamberlain oversaw food and drink; and the steward ran the estates and finances.

TALL TOWERS
San Gimignano, Italy, is an extreme example of what happened when rival families clashed. Here 72 tall castles were built in the same town, of which 14 survive today.

OLD AND NEW
Castle walls or buildings were often repaired or replaced, to take advantage of new defensive ideas. At Falaise, France, the castle was given a square tower by Henry I in the 12th century and a round one by King Philip Augustus in the early 13th century.

Natural rocky outcrop provides base for castle

ANCESTOR
At Mycenae, Greece, a strong fortified palace was built in about 1250 B.C. The Lion Gate guards the entrance. Such a state-run building is not a true castle, even though it has large stone fortifications.

IRON AGE
The large earthworks at Maiden castle, England, are actually the remains of a Celtic palisaded (fenced) settlement built on a New Stone Age site. It was really more like a fortified town than a castle and was captured by the Romans.

MASTER
This early 14th-century picture shows a king instructing a master mason, who was in charge of the castle's construction. He carries a set square. Some kings built numerous castles but lived in them only occasionally.

SYMBOL OF POWER
As well as being a home, the castle was a symbol of power. Caernarfon in North Wales, begun together with a walled town in 1283, was one of a series of castles built by Edward I of England in order to impress the people of Wales.

Main stone tower on top of mound

Inner curtain wall

TURKISH TOWERS
Van castle in Turkey was begun in A.D. 850. During the Middle Ages it was repaired by the Seljuk and Ottoman Turks, and was later lived in by Armenian Christians.

Steep crag makes castle difficult to attack

MEETING PLACE
Castles were often the scenes of important meetings about state affairs. This picture shows the meeting of Richard II and his uncle the Duke of Gloucester that took place at Pleshey castle.

The first castles

THE EARLIEST CASTLES appeared in the 9th and 10th centuries, when the empire created by Charlemagne in modern France, Germany, and northern Italy was collapsing as a result of raids by peoples such as Vikings and Magyars (Hungarian nomads). Lords built castles for protection and as bases for their soldiers. Most of these early castles were built of earth and timber. The simplest was the ringwork: an enclosure surrounded by a ditch with an earth rampart inside it. A strong fence (or palisade) was built on the rampart. In the 11th century motte-and-bailey castles became popular. An earth mound (or motte) was built next to a yard (or bailey).

BUILDING A MOTTE
The Bayeux Tapestry, probably made between 1066 and 1086, shows a motte being built at Hastings, England, by the Normans. The motte is being made of rammed layers of soil, although no evidence of this method has been found in the real motte at Hastings.

LAST REMAINS
A motte with two baileys was built at Yelden, England, probably soon after the Norman conquest. The ditches were fed by a local stream. Often a grassy mound like this is all that remains of an early castle.

Thatched roof

Hall

Stables

Bailey

Wood palisade

Lifting bridge

Castle yard or bailey — *Earth motte*

TIMBER TOWER
This stylized picture of a motte comes from the Bayeux Tapestry. It is supposed to show the castle at Rennes, the former capital of Brittany. The wooden palisade around the top encloses a wooden tower. If it were not for pictures like this, we would not know what these towers looked like.

PLESHEY
The large motte-and-bailey at Pleshey, England, was built by the Normans soon after 1066. This type of castle could be erected in a matter of months rather than years, which was ideal when the Normans were in a hostile country. Pleshey castle has one motte and one bailey, but sometimes there were two mottes or two baileys.

MOTTE-AND-BAILEY STYLE
These castles were built in the 11th and 12th centuries. There was a bailey or courtyard, protected by a ditch and palisade, and an entrance gate often with a lifting bridge, a drawbridge, or even a gate tower. Within the bailey were stables and workshops, a well, and perhaps a chapel. The motte was the final refuge. Many mottes were only about 15 ft (5 m) high, but some were twice that size. The tower on top was usually of wood – stone towers were often too heavy for artificial mounds. Some towers had many rooms, but if there was only space for a watchtower on the motte, a great hall might be built in the bailey.

Roof of wooden shingles

Wood stilts to give space under tower

Wooden walkway

Motte, or earth mound

Wooden flying (overhead) bridge

The great tower

DURING THE 10TH CENTURY lords began to build castles out of stone. A large stone tower could become the main military and residential building of a castle. Because the towers were expensive to build and took a long time to erect, and because skilled masons (stoneworkers) were needed to plan and build them, few such towers were built until the 11th century. They are now often known as keeps, but in their day they were called great towers or donjons. The Normans liked great towers with massively thick stone walls, and they built several after their conquest of England in 1066. Many more were built in the next century. Stone towers were stronger than wooden walls and did not burn. Attackers had to use other ways to destroy them, such as chipping away at the corners with picks, or digging tunnels beneath (undermining) the foundations to weaken them.

PRISON
Great towers had many different uses. Here the Duke of Orleans, captured by the English at the Battle of Agincourt in 1415, awaits his ransom. He is held in the White Tower, in the middle of the Tower of London.

HOARDINGS
Built in about 1150, the octagonal tower at Provins, France, is shown here with wooden hoardings (pp. 28–29) that were added later.

SHELL
As stone defenses became more common, the wooden palisades around the top of a motte (pp. 8–9) were sometimes replaced with stone walls for added strength. Structures like this are now called shell keeps. This ring-work (low stone wall) at Restormel, Cornwall, also has low stone walls and provides a roomy courtyard within the walls.

Double windows provide more light

GREAT HALL
One floor of the great tower of Hedingham castle was used as the great hall, in which the lord and his household lived and ate. To light the hall, large alcoves were set into the walls. Doors in some of the alcoves lead to lavatories or rooms called mural chambers. The level above has a gallery recessed into the wall, and it runs the length of the hall.

Window in alcove

Zigzag decoration, typical of buildings of the 12th century

KEEPING WARM
In wooden buildings the fire was made in an open hearth in the middle of the floor. But with a stone tower fireplaces could be built into the thickness of the wall. The flue passed through the wall to the outside and carried much of the smoke away from the room.

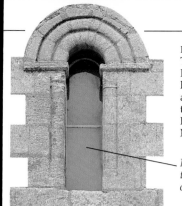

ROUND HEAD
The windows at Hedingham all have round arches typical of the style called Romanesque, or Norman.

Narrow opening to stop the entry of arrows

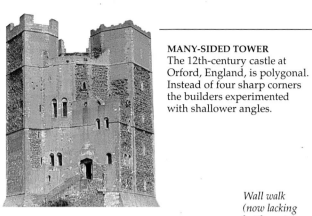

MANY-SIDED TOWER
The 12th-century castle at Orford, England, is polygonal. Instead of four sharp corners the builders experimented with shallower angles.

Flag of castle owner

Wall walk (now lacking battlements)

HEDINGHAM CASTLE
The great tower at Hedingham, England, was built in about 1140 by Aubrey de Vere. It is not a large keep but still has the interior strengthened by an arch on the first and second floors. The doorway was originally protected by a stone forebuilding, but only part of this has survived.

Stair turret, also used as a watchtower

Finely cut facing stone (ashlar)

Quarters for the lord's family

Gallery of the great hall

Great hall

Brick and rubble infill

Door to entrance floor, probably also garrison (troops) quarters

Surviving lower portion of stone forebuilding

Concentric castles

CONQUERING KING
Edward I was a great builder of castles in North Wales.

From THE MID 13TH CENTURY, castles were built with rings of stone walls, one inside the other. These are called concentric castles. The outer wall was fairly close to and lower than the inner, sometimes so low that it seemed no more than a barrier against siege machines (such as catapults). But it meant that archers on the inner walls could shoot over the heads of those on the outer, bringing twice the fire power to bear on an enemy. If attackers broke through the outer wall, they would still be faced with the inner wall. Some towers could be sealed off, leaving the enemy exposed on the wall walks of the outer wall. In older castles the great tower and curtain wall were sometimes given an outer ring of walls, making three lines of defense.

GATEHOUSE
This is the gatehouse on a dam wall which leads to the outer eastern gate at Caerphilly castle. The twin holes above the archway are for the chains of a lifting bridge. Behind this were a portcullis and double-doors. Notice the "spurs" which jut out to strengthen the base of each tower.

Putlog holes to take wood supports for hoardings

Gatehouse

Round corner tower

Outer curtain wall

Leaning tower

Artificial lake

LET THERE BE LIGHT
This is not an arrow loop but a window in Caerphilly castle, large enough to allow light and air through to the rooms inside. Even so, windows might have iron grilles to keep out intruders. Glass was rare, and shutters were used in bad weather.

Iron grille

WATER DEFENSES
Probably inspired by Kenilworth castle, England, Caerphilly sits in a huge artificial lake, formed by damming a stream. The lake prevented attempts to tunnel under the walls and forced siege machines to keep their distance.

High inner wall

EDWARDIAN CASTLE
Edward I of England built many huge castles in North Wales to try and control the hostile Welsh. Beaumaris, built on the island of Anglesey, was the last. Planned during a revolt in 1294, which was put down two years later, the concentric defenses became unnecessary and building stopped in 1300, never to be completed.

CAERPHILLY
Caerphilly castle in South Wales was built mainly between 1268 and 1271 by Gilbert de Clare during his struggles with the Welsh prince Llewellyn ap Gruffydd. It is the earliest regular concentric castle in Britain and the largest castle in Wales. The western gatehouse defends the outer walls. Behind it rise the higher inner walls with strong corner towers. The doors to the inner gatehouse from the wall walk could be protected against enemies by portcullises.

Low outer wall

Arrow loop

Window with metal bars

Crenellations

Inner curtain wall

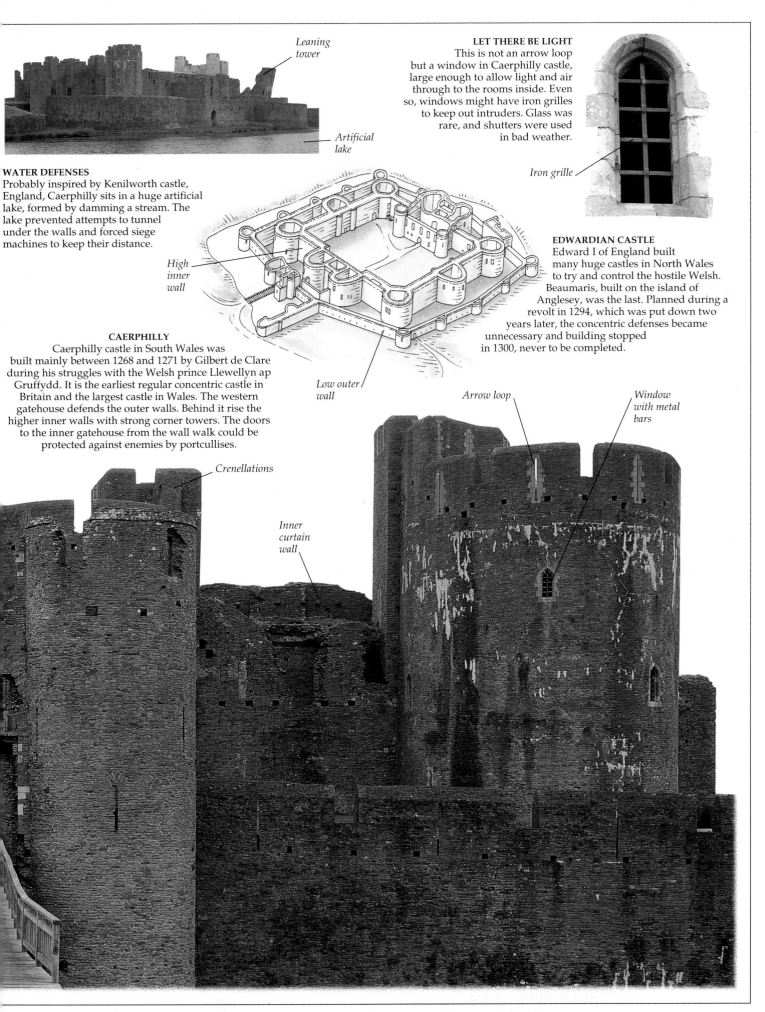

Castles on the Loire

MANY CASTLES were built along the Loire River in France. Doue-La-Fontaine, probably the oldest known keep, was one of the first. French castles developed during the reign of Philip Augustus (1180-1226) with powerful keeps, enclosures, round towers, and towers *en bec* (like a beak) on which the outward-facing side is drawn out like a ship's prow. Flying turrets jutted from walls without reaching the ground, and towers often had tall, conical roofs. In the 15th century, French castles became more luxurious.

Polychrome jug

Floor tiles

FRENCH TASTES
The 14th-century polychrome (many-colored) jug is in typical French style. The floor tiles are from Saumur castle and bear heraldic pictures. The fleur-de-lys was used in French royal arms and became the symbol of the French royal house. It therefore appeared in the coats of arms of a number of people related to the royal family.

Rope for hauling bucket

Wooden teeth

Wooden cog wheel

Strong wooden framework

Crank handle

WINDER
At Saumur, water could be brought up from an underground well using these winding wheels. The wheels are made of wood and the teeth of one mesh with holes in the other.

LORDS AND LADIES
French nobles always felt themselves to be among the leaders of fashion, and French courts were the centers of elegance. These lords and ladies of the turn of the 16th century are dressed in expensive robes.

ENTRANCE
Stone steps now lead up to the entrance at Saumur, which is flanked on either side by flying turrets. The machicolations (openings) in the middle allowed materials to be dropped on enemies attacking the gate. On the right, a concave ramp enables goods to be dragged or barrels rolled up or down it.

SAUMUR *right*
Saumur castle may have been begun as early as the 10th century but has been rebuilt several times. By the 15th century it had a fairy-tale appearance, complete with golden weathercocks, as shown in a picture from the Duke of Berry's book, *Les très riches heures*. It became a comfortable residence but was abandoned in the 17th century when the west wing fell down. It was then used as a prison and barracks but was later restored.

THE VINEYARDS

The illustration of September from the Duke of Berry's *Les très riches heures,* written in about 1416, shows the grape harvest in the vineyard below the whitewashed walls of Saumur castle. The lower windows have iron grilles to stop people from getting in. The upper parts, although machicolated, have fantastic Gothic-style carved traceries (ornamental bars). The barbican (outer) gate has both a small and large lifting bridge. On its left are small jutting latrine blocks which drop waste into ditches. To their left is the tall chimney of the kitchen, isolated to guard against spreading fire.

Stair tower

Well house

WELL

The courtyard at Saumur has a well with a large underground water tank. This tank extends under the covered well house on the left, which contains the winding mechanism for lifting large buckets.

Corner tower

Stair turret with conical roof

Machicolations

Castles in Spain

SHIP OF STONE
The Alcazar (palace) of Segovia, rebuilt in the early 15th century, is called a *gran buque,* or "great ship" castle because of its long shape. The earlier keep was separated from the new tower-keep.

Sᴘᴀɪɴ ʜᴀᴅ ᴍᴜsʟɪᴍ rulers (the Moors) from A.ᴅ. 711 until Christians took their last stronghold, Granada, in 1492. The Muslims built a different style of fort from the Christians; most common were square or wedge-shaped towered *alcazabas* (garrison forts). Their enemies, the Christian knights, built *torres del homenaje* (tower-keeps) which were often round. From the 14th century on, the Christians pushed south; building castles more like those found in England and France. Later, conflicts between king and nobles led to a style of fort that mixed Moorish and Christian styles.

Decorative false machicolations mimic the real thing but have no gaps for dropping missiles

Ball decoration

Crenellated corner tower

Coat-of-arms

Arrow slit

16

A SIEGE
The wall-towers are packed with soldiers in this 13th-century Spanish wall fresco of an attack on Majorca. On the right, a staff sling is about to be released. This sling was attached to a wooden pole which extended the range its stone or lead bullet could be hurled.

Octagonal turret

CASTLE PALACE
Heavily influenced by Moorish styles, *el Real de Manzanares*, north of Madrid, was built in 1435 for a powerful duke. It is almost square in shape and is surrounded with two sets of walls with round towers. In 1480 the next duke added the gallery, turret, and ball decoration.

ALL A GAME
The Moors lived in Spain after they conquered it in the 8th century. They established a civilization there which in many ways was well in advance of Christian Europe. From the 10th century on Christians, including religious orders of monk-knights, tried to seize Spain from the Moors. Here two Moors play a form of chess.

GRANADA
In 1492 the town of Granada in southern Spain, the last Moorish stronghold in Spain, fell to the Christians. The Alhambra is a fortified palace set on a nearby hill and is full of the most beautiful Moorish decoration, like these graceful arches around a courtyard.

Ornate gallery

Inner curtain wall

Outer curtain wall

Castles in Germany

IN WHAT IS NOW GERMANY, many princes and nobles lived in castles under the leadership of an emperor. As central control broke down in the 13th century, many lesser lords also built castles, some as bases for robbery. German castle design was often influenced by the land. Many castles took advantage of hills and mountains; others were built along the banks of the Rhine River. In flatter areas the *Wasserburg*, a type of castle protected by a wide moat, was seen. The Teutonic Order of monk-knights built brick castles like blockhouses (structures for defense), containing residential and religious areas set around a rectangular courtyard. Most large 11th- and 12th-century castles were later given a curtain wall with flanking towers.

LONG OCCUPATION
Schloss Mespelbrunn at Spessart, Bavaria, began as a medieval castle and was rebuilt in the 16th century to suit the taste for more comfort. Because the castle sits in a huge moat, its builders could put large windows in the outer walls.

POTTERY
This type of pottery is known as Rhenish ware because it was made in the Rhineland. It was often exported to other countries. These jugs would have been "thrown" on a potter's wheel and partly glazed to add color.

Handle

Spout

Hollow body for water

HILLTOP HOME
Cochem castle sits on a hill overlooking the Moselle River. It was probably begun in about 1020. The tall *Bergfried*, or tower, is typically German. The castle was used as a toll station, and there was a chain to bar the river.

LION JUG
The aquamanile was a type of metal or pottery jug that had a spout to pour water for washing hands at mealtimes. Different forms of aquamanile were made, including jugs in the shape of knights on horseback. This German copper-alloy lion has a man sitting astride its back, pulling its ears.

WAY IN
The entrance to the castle of Pfalzgrafenstein is guarded by a wooden portcullis sheathed in iron. Instead of moving up and down slots within the gate passage, the portcullis is set against the wall and slides through slots cut in stone brackets. Above the lifting chains are the curved arches of machicolations. On the right of the gate is an opening protected by a wooden shutter.

ISLAND CASTLE
The five-sided tower of the Pfalzgrafenstein was built as a toll-station on an island in the Rhine by King Ludwig I of Bavaria in 1327.

THE ENCLOSURE
This view from the tower of the Pfalzgrafenstein shows the domestic buildings set against the inner side of the enclosure walls. A covered wooden gallery runs alongside these buildings. In the middle is one of the circular turrets which covers the angle where two walls meet.

Belfry on medieval tower

A CASTLE RE-USED
The hexagonal enclosure of the Pfalzgrafenstein was added between about 1338 and 1342 to create a turret fortress, a type of castle typical of western Germany. Useful even after the end of the Middle Ages, it was strengthened further in 1607, when one end was given a protruding bastion.

Gun ports

HOME COMFORTS
The latrine, or toilet, has a wooden seat to give added comfort.

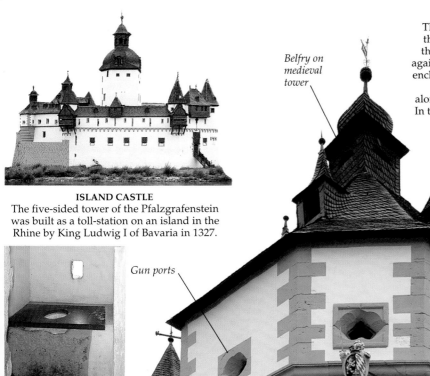

Window

Wooden hoarding for defence

Seventeenth-century bastion

Continued on next page

FLOOR TILE
This tile came from the Marksburg. It shows how lords tried to brighten up what must have been rather cold and uncomfortable rooms.

LOOK TO HEAVEN
The painted ceiling of the chapel in the Marksburg gives some idea of the type of interior decoration used. Like many German castles, this one had small, homely rooms rather than great halls.

Castles on crags

In some areas, especially in Germany, castle-builders took advantage of hilly or mountainous countryside. The steepness made assault by men or war machines difficult, and rock foundations deterred mining. When central control broke down in Germany in the mid-13th century and many of the lesser German barons built castles, they found that one of the cheapest ways was to circle the top of a crag (rugged cliff) with a wall. This wall was often rebuilt with flanking towers. A deep ditch was dug on the weakest side, or a very high mantle wall erected. If all sides needed equal protection, the walls might surround a central tower. Otherwise the domestic buildings were fortified and set around the courtyard to form a type of castle called a *Randhausburg*.

GROWING CASTLE
The central tower of the Marksburg, near the Rhine in Germany, dates from the early Middle Ages and has gradually been surrounded by defenses built later. It has small French-style flying turrets, but the arched friezes rising above the walls are typical of the Rhineland.

Glazed earthenware cooking pot

Barred door

Metal skimmer

Flue rises through thickness of castle wall

Flat-bottomed iron pot

Ladle

WALL SPACE
This niche in the wall has been given a shelf and filled with jugs behind a barred door.

BUILDING WORK
This German illustration portrays the Biblical story of the Tower of Babel. Although the tower was supposed to have been built long before the Medieval period, these workers are using methods that German builders would have used to construct a castle.

WELCOME GLOW
Food was cooked over the kitchen fire in medieval castles (see pp. 40–41). This kitchen fireplace in Pfalzgrafenstein has a metal cooking pot hanging over the fire. Pots and bowls stand ready on the shelf above, and a metal ladle and a skimmer hang to one side. Because kitchens had fires, there was always a possible danger. Sometimes the kitchen was put in a separate building; sometimes it was separated from the great hall by a passage, which gave some added safety.

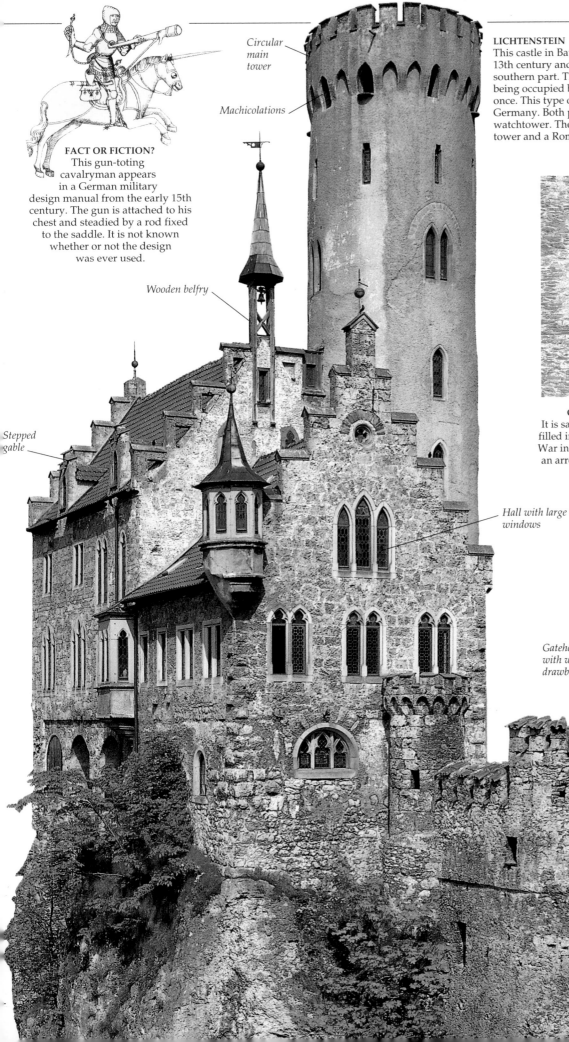

FACT OR FICTION?
This gun-toting cavalryman appears in a German military design manual from the early 15th century. The gun is attached to his chest and steadied by a rod fixed to the saddle. It is not known whether or not the design was ever used.

Circular main tower

Machicolations

Wooden belfry

Stepped gable

LICHTENSTEIN
This castle in Bavaria was begun in the early 13th century and is divided into a northern and a southern part. This layout is the result of the castle being occupied by several members of a family at once. This type of fortification is sometimes seen in Germany. Both parts have a square or rectangular watchtower. The northern section also has a round tower and a Romanesque chapel.

CHANGING NEEDS
It is said that this window was filled in during the Thirty Years War in the 17th century, leaving an arrow loop to shoot from in times of trouble.

Hall with large windows

Gatehouse with wooden drawbridge

The chapel

The dead were wrapped in cloth shrouds. A coffin was often used to take a dead body to the grave.

THE CHAPEL WAS an important room in a Christian castle, because inhabitants were expected to join in regular services. In early towers the chapel was often on the top floor or in an upper room in the entrance building. As castles developed, the chapel became part of the domestic range of buildings. It might be decorated with carved stonework and wall paintings that often illustrated a Bible story, because few people could read the Bible itself and so many relied on pictures. The clergy were among the few who could read and write and so, in addition to their religious duties, they looked after the documents relating to the castle. A chaplain therefore often had several clerks to help him.

FAITH AND POLITICS
This 15th-century illustration shows Thomas Arundel, archbishop of Canterbury, England, preaching the cause of Henry IV. Banished by Richard II, Henry IV landed in England in 1399 with Thomas and, supported by a group of nobles, seized the crown. Medieval churchmen were often mixed up with political intrigues. Bishops did not work in castle chapels; the most powerful of them held castles in their own right.

ROYAL CUP
The Royal Gold Cup was made in about 1380 for the Duke of Berry in France and has been in the possession of both English and French kings. It is decorated in colored enamels with scenes of saints' lives – religious teaching was always present in every medieval household.

Scene of the adoration of the Magi

Magi awakened by an angel

TEACHING IN STONE
The entrance to the chapel at the castle of Loches in France dates from the late 12th century. The doorway is carved with figures which were designed to help teach people who were unable to read.

Statue of a bishop

Carvings of animals and mythical beasts

Saint Peter

Holy water stoup

Sword with broad,
diamond-sectioned blade

Gauntlet

Priest
attending
Becket

This miter (bishop's hat)
was probably Becket's

SEAL
Becket's seal shows an
early miter worn side-on.
Later bishops, like
Thomas Arundel on the
opposite page, wore their
miters front-on, as
bishops do today.

*Thomas
Becket in
prayer at
the altar*

Poleyn

MARTYRDOM
This piece of alabaster
is carved with a scene
of the death of Thomas
Becket in 1170, though the
knights all wear armor of
the late 14th century,
when the carving was
made. Becket
was archbishop of
Canterbury under Henry
II of England, but the two
men constantly argued.
After an angry outburst
by Henry, four knights
murdered Becket in
his own cathedral.
He was soon hailed as
a saint and Canterbury
became a great shrine
for pilgrims.

Laying a siege

I<small>F SURROUNDING</small> a castle and trying to starve the defenders into submission did not work, attackers could try to take it by force. They could tunnel under the walls to topple them, or come up inside the courtyard. Defenders might place bowls of water on the ground so that any tunneling activity made the water ripple. Then they could dig countermines to break into the tunnels, leading to a fierce struggle underground. Attackers might also try to break down the walls using artillery or battering rams slung under movable sheds. Defenders lowered hooks to catch the heads of battering rams, or dropped mattresses to cushion the blows. A direct assault over the walls meant using scaling ladders to hook onto battlements; this was dangerous as defenders pushed them away from the walls with forked poles.

CHIPPING AWAY
Under cover of a shed on wheels, miners pick away stones at the wall base. Wooden props were then inserted and burned to make the wall collapse.

Wheel to move shield

MOVABLE SHIELD
Archers and crossbowmen used these shields to protect themselves while trying to pick off defenders and covering assaults.

PEOPLE POWER
The traction trebuchet, which probably appeared in the mid-12th century, had a team of men hauling on ropes at the short end of a beam, so pivoting up the other end with its sling. This opened to release a large stone.

Ropes for hauling

Sling

Pivoting arm

MOUTHPIECE
From the 12th century, heralds were used to demand surrender on their lord's behalf. They wore the lord's coat of arms for recognition.

Counterweight

Large stones for use as missiles

HEAVYWEIGHT
The counterpoise trebuchet, which probably appeared in the late 12th century, used a huge box of earth and stones instead of manpower to pull down the arm and send a missile flying into the air.

Winch

KEEP YOUR HEAD UP
Severed enemy heads were sometimes thrown to demoralize the opposition. Messengers with rejected terms might be trussed up in a trebuchet, or dung or dead animals thrown to spread disease.

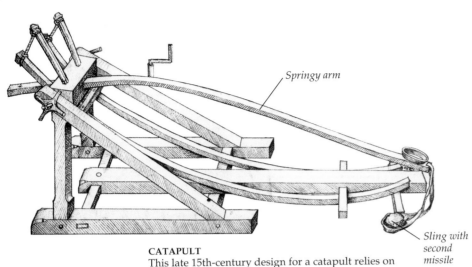

CATAPULT
This late 15th-century design for a catapult relies on springy arms to throw the missile. Another type of catapult, the mangon, had been in use since Roman times. It used the tension created by a wooden beam placed between twisted ropes or hair to hurl large stones through the air.

Springy arm

Sling with second missile

HEAVE!
A team of men haul on ropes to pull down the arm of a traction trebuchet. The operators (or gynours) were probably always within bowshot, and needed to be protected by palisades. Large machines were made on site. Catapults were also used by defenders to destroy the besieger's machines.

A wooden tower is used to watch over a besieged castle

Sliding section of tiller

Ratchet for keeping tension on skeins

Skein of twisted ropes

Bolt

Bow cord

GIANT CROSSBOW
The ballista had been in use since the time of the ancient Greeks. It used twisted ropes that held the two arms of a huge crossbow. Some medieval forms used the tension of a single large bow arm. A winch, or sometimes a wooden screw, pulled back the sliding tiller to draw the cord. The ballista was an anti-personnel weapon. It was used to discourage sorties (when defenders would rush out of the castle and mount a surprise attack on their enemies); with it, defenders could pick off attackers.

Wooden wheel, reinforced with metal

Men and missiles

CASTLES HAD SPECIAL features to protect the defenders while allowing them to shoot at their enemies. Battlements and loopholes enabled archers to cover a wide area in front of the castle. The gaps (or crenels) in the battlements were sometimes fitted with shutters to deflect missiles. The stone parts of the battlements (the merlons) might also have loopholes for archers to shoot through. To guard against missiles, surprise attacks (sorties) by the garrison, and assault by relief forces, besiegers might surround their lines with palisades. Sometimes they moved on but left a timber "siege castle" full of men to watch the castle.

OVER THE WATER
Some castles had a wet moat or lake and others were built near a river or the seashore. Occasionally besiegers brought up boats that contained scaling ladders or even wooden towers from which they tried to cross the walls.

NARROW LOOPHOLES
These holes were usually splayed on the inside to form an embrasure, or open chamber, within the wall. The archer probably stood just to one side of this, looking through the hole until an enemy came within range. Then he would move to the center of the embrasure to shoot. Enemy marksmen may have gotten some arrows through loopholes, especially if shooting at close range.

Crank handle

Pulley

Windlass cord

WINDLASS
Some crossbows were so powerful that a windlass was needed to draw back the thick cord attached to the bow-arm. Turning the handles wound up the windlass cords which were attached by hooks to the cord of the bow. Pulleys reduced the effort needed to pull the cord.

Crossbow cord

Bow arm

Wooden shaft

Feather flight

ARROWS
The longbow came to prominence in the 12th century. It could propel its arrows at least 1,000 ft (300 m). A longbowman could shoot about 12 arrows in the time it took to load a crossbow, but the strength needed to pull the bow meant that they needed regular practice.

Leather flight

Knock to take bow string

Stirrup

QUARREL *below*
Crossbows shot short arrows called bolts. Because of their four-sided heads they were also known as quarrels, from *carre*, the old French word for "four."

Wooden shaft

Iron point

Cord drawn back

Bow arm

Tiller

Stirrup

Bolt

Every medieval soldier would carry a dagger, ready at his waist in case he had to take part in hand-to-hand combat

THE CROSSBOW
Crossbows were powerful but slow to reload. For this reason their use in a castle was ideal, because the crossbowman could prepare his weapon from behind the safety of the walls. In some cases a second crossbow might be loaded by an assistant while the crossbowman was aiming the first one, so speeding up the process.

GOING UP
Spiral staircases were common in medieval castles. Each stair ended in a circular slab and the next stair was laid with this end over the one below, so creating the cylindrical newel post (center column). Such stairs often spiral up in a clockwise direction; this may have been deliberately done to hamper an attacker fighting his way up the stairs, whose weapon (in his right hand) would keep hitting the stonework.

SURRENDER
The burghers (middle class) of Calais, France, surrender to the English king Edward III in 1340. The victor received the keys of the stronghold. Defenders who refused to surrender immediately faced looting, pillage, and death if they were defeated.

SHIELDED
Besieging crossbowmen also needed protection when reloading.

Tricks of defense

THE FIRST OBSTACLE faced by someone attacking a castle was a wet or dry moat. A moat made it difficult for attackers to bring siege machines near the castle. If dry, stakes might be planted to slow an enemy and make him an easier target. The gatehouse was an obvious weak spot, so a *barbican*, or defensive work, was sometimes placed in front to guard the approach. A drawbridge and portcullis gave extra protection. The portcullis was an iron-covered wooden grille moving up and down in slots on either side of the entrance passage. It was raised by a winch in a room above and could be dropped quickly if danger threatened. Drawbridges over the ditch took several forms, including simple wooden platforms which were pulled back, lifting bridges attached by chains to pulleys, and turning bridges pivoted like a seesaw.

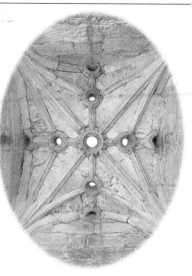

DROPPING IN
The gate passage at Bodiam has so-called "murder holes" (*meutrières*) in the roof so cold water could be poured down to put out fires. Also scalding water, hot sand, or other offensive substances might be dropped on enemies who managed to get in.

GATEHOUSE
This castle's passage is flanked by huge towers. Missiles could be dropped on an attacker through slots over the arch.

FLARING BASE
The Castel Nuovo ("new castle") in Naples, Italy, has a *chemise*, or small outer wall. This wall has a splayed-out base (called a batter or talus), so that missiles dropped from above bounce out toward the enemy. It also thickened the wall, giving added protection against attacks by battering rams, undermining, or bombardment. The castle was rebuilt in the years 1442-1458 as an early experiment against artillery, so this example was also designed to deflect enemy cannon balls.

Curtain wall

Corbel supporting machicolated parapet

Batter or talus

GUN-PORT
In the late 14th century keyhole-shaped gun-ports appeared. Round ports were usually for handguns while horizontal slots were for small cannon mounted behind walls. This example is from the Pfalzgrafenstein in Germany.

MACHICOLATIONS
Machicolations were stone versions of wooden hoardings and developed in the 12th century. The battlements jutted beyond the walls and were supported on stone corbels. Gaps left between the corbels allowed offensive material to be dropped on enemies at the wall base.

STICKING OUT
The Pfalzgrafenstein on the Rhine has a number of hoardings built out from the tops of its walls. These are wooden constructions with gaps in the floor allowing defenders to drop missiles on attackers at the foot of the wall without having to expose themselves by leaning out over the battlements. Hot water, red-hot sand, or rocks might be thrown, as well as quicklime. Boiling oil, beloved of film-makers, is rarely mentioned.

Steep roof to throw off missiles

Slots for observation and shooting through

Wooden walls

Timber support

LIFTING BRIDGES
The *bascule* bridge had chains attached to wooden beams weighted at the rear. This end dropped when released, lifting the front of the bridge into recesses in the wall.

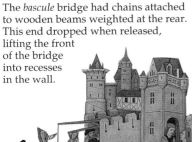

Manuscript showing lifting bridge with wooden beams and chains

Pedestrian and main lifting bridges at Langeais, France

Machicolated parapet

Turret for observation

CURTAINS AND FLANKS
The 14th-century castle at Bodiam, England, has stretches of curtain walls protected by flanking towers which jut out beyond the wall face.

Round tower, less vulnerable to miners than sharp angles

Loophole

The garrison

Basinet

Mail curtain
(or aventail)

Steel
gauntlet

Jupon

THE BODY OF SOLDIERS who lived in a castle and defended it was called the garrison. In early castles, especially at times of unrest, these men might be knights who lived permanently in their lord's castle. In return for accommodation they fought for the lord and guarded the castle. Gradually more knights settled on their own estates, and the knightly duties were done using a rotation system. A knight stayed in the castle for a set period, then he was replaced by another man. During the 14th and 15th centuries it became more common for hired soldiers to guard castles, although this tended to increase the fear of betrayal.

Part of
shield

UNDER SIEGE
The garrison was vital in times of siege. In this German manuscript of the early 14th century the women of the castle help out the hard-pressed defenders.

HORSE DECOR
In the 14th and 15th centuries the bridle and breast straps of horses were often decorated with enameled pendants made of copper-alloy. This one bears the arms of the Berkeley family.

MAN OF STEEL
By the later 14th century, as shown by this stone figure of St. George, a knight's limbs were often enclosed in steel plates and a coat of plates was worn under a tight quilted or cloth garment called a jupon. The steel helmet, called a basinet, is fitted with a curtain of mail to protect the sides of the head and neck. This figure carries a shield, though these were becoming less common by this time.

KNIGHTLY DUTIES
Castles usually had only a small garrison in peacetime, and
even in times of trouble soldiers were usually counted in tens rather
than in hundreds. The garrison provided a ready supply of knights,
men-at-arms, and squires when a lord needed them. Armed men were
needed not only in time of war. Lords used armed men as escorts to
protect them on the roads, especially from robbers in wooded areas. In
this 14th-century picture the arrival of armored men is greeted by
fanfares from the castle.

Loop for chain

Dragon emblem

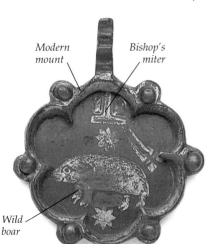

Round-topped shield, typically Italian in shape

Modern mount

Bishop's miter

Arms of Cresci family

Wild boar

DRAGON
This badge
dates from the
15th century and
depicts a dragon.
This creature was a
common emblem in
heraldry. The badge is
decorated with enamel,
and was worn as a pendant.

Worn white enamel decoration

MEDALLION
This silver medallion comes from Florence,
Italy, and dates from the 14th century. The
right-hand shield may show the arms of the
Cresci family, suggesting that it could have
belonged to one of that family's retainers.

OLD BOAR
This 15th-century horse pendant was,
like the others, cast in copper-alloy and
decorated with enamel. The decoration
shows a wild boar and a bishop's miter.
The pendant has been cut down
and mounted.

MULBERRY BUSH
This badge of a mulberry bush
belonged to a retainer of the Mowbray
family. Followers of noble families often
wore metal badges like this, or cloth
badges stitched to their clothing
for identification.

FIGHTING MAN
Knights who garrisoned
Norman castles had coats of
mail, steel helmets, and
large wooden shields.

THORN IN THE SIDE
Castles were not just
fortified dwellings. They
were bases from which
soldiers controlled the
surrounding countryside.
This meant that an
invader of an area first
had to attack the local
castles, or run the risk of
his supply lines being cut.

The castle as prison

Welsh prince Gruffydd falls to his death trying to escape from the Tower of London in 1244

A CASTLE SEEMS AN IDEAL PLACE for keeping prisoners. In medieval times most prisoners were political or state prisoners. Some of them were captured noblemen awaiting the payment of ransom money. They were given good living conditions, because they were valueless to their captors if they died. Such men might even give their word of honor not to escape, in return for some freedom. Most rooms called "dungeons" were probably cellars – only the ones with difficult access may have been prisons. These were sometimes called *oubliettes*, a French word suggesting that the prisoners were left and forgotten. Criminals were not imprisoned in castles in the Middle Ages. They were usually punished by fine, mutilation, or execution. More castles were used as prisons after the Middle Ages. In fact, most stories involving torture, imprisonment, and execution taking place in castles belong after the Middle Ages, in the 17th and 18th centuries.

MANACLES
This iron collar is attached to a chain, which was in turn secured to the wall of a room in Loches castle. To add to the discomfort, the collar weighs about 35 lb (16 kg). Few men of rank would be kept in such conditions.

Locking iron ring

Heavy iron chain attached to wall

GOOD KING RICHARD?
The English king Richard III was said to have ordered the murder of his two nephews, Edward V and Richard, in the Tower of London in 1483. The princes were kept in the Tower to prevent nobles from using them as rivals for the throne. Nobody knows who really killed them or exactly when they died.

Part of castle containing prison

Barred window

A PRISON
The keep at Loches, France, was used as a prison from the 15th century on. This example, together with a few others such as the Tower of London, seem to imply that blood and death were common in such places. But most stories of prisoners' misery belong in later times, when castles were used for political executions or as common jails.

VAULTS
A post at Chillon castle, France, has an iron ring attached, to which prisoners were manacled to prevent them from escaping.

VICTIM?
This picture shows Edward V with his parents Edward IV and Elizabeth Woodville.

DEATH BY BURNING
Those who refused to follow the state religion were sometimes burned at the stake. Many burnings took place during the 16th century.

OFF WITH HIS HEAD!
The sword was used in Europe for beheading, as in this picture of 1415. The victim waits blindfolded for the fatal blow.

Banner bearing fleur-de-lys, the traditional heraldic symbol of France

MAID OF ORLEANS
This 19th-century statue is of Joan of Arc, a young Frenchwoman from Orleans who was burned at the stake for witchcraft in 1431 because of her leading role in victories over the English. She was imprisoned in the castle at Rouen during her trial.

Stout grille made of hard wood

Wooden peg

Window

Stone bench seat

Small wooden door for passing food and drink to prisoner inside

BARRED VIEW
A strong wooden grille confines the prisoner in his room in the castle at Loches. Prisoners were often allowed to have much more space than in this small cell.

Crusader castles

FOR OVER 200 YEARS European Christians fought the Muslims to try to win control of the Holy Land by launching expeditions called Crusades. They were impressed by huge Byzantine and Muslim fortifications and took over Muslim strongholds to encourage European settlers. They built castles to guard roads and to help them attack nearby towns. By the late 12th century such castles were being used as border posts, administrative centers, safe havens, and army bases. Often, the Crusaders used ideal sites for castles, places protected on three sides by a sea or river; they built strong walls and ditches to guard the fourth side. When, rapid building was necessary, so simple rectangular enclosures with corner and flanking towers were raised.

BESIEGED
This 13th-century Italian manuscript shows Crusaders trying to break into Antioch. This city was so large that the men of the First Crusade (1095–1099) could not surround it, in spite of the size of their army. So they had to guard against sorties (p. 25) from the gates, building forts to watch over them. European artists knew that the crescent was a Muslim symbol, and thought it was used on the defenders' shields.

MAILED KNIGHT
Crusaders, like this knight of about 1280, wore a shirt of mail, a cloth surcoat, and a helm on the head.

Battlements

Main tower

Small window

POOR KNIGHTS?
The seal of the Knights Templar shows two knights on one horse, suggesting their original poverty. This order of warrior-monks was formed in 1119. They took their name from their headquarters, which was near the Temple in Jerusalem.

KERAK
This castle stands on a narrow neck of land in the Jordanian desert. It is isolated from the nearby town, and from the approach at the other end, by ditches cut in the rock. The other sides have natural, steep rock slopes. A lower courtyard on one side gave the defenders two levels from which to fire. Built in 1142, it was so effective in disrupting the communications of the Muslims that it was attacked several times. It took an eight-month siege by the Muslim leader Saladin in 1188 before the castle fell.

Wall of lower courtyard

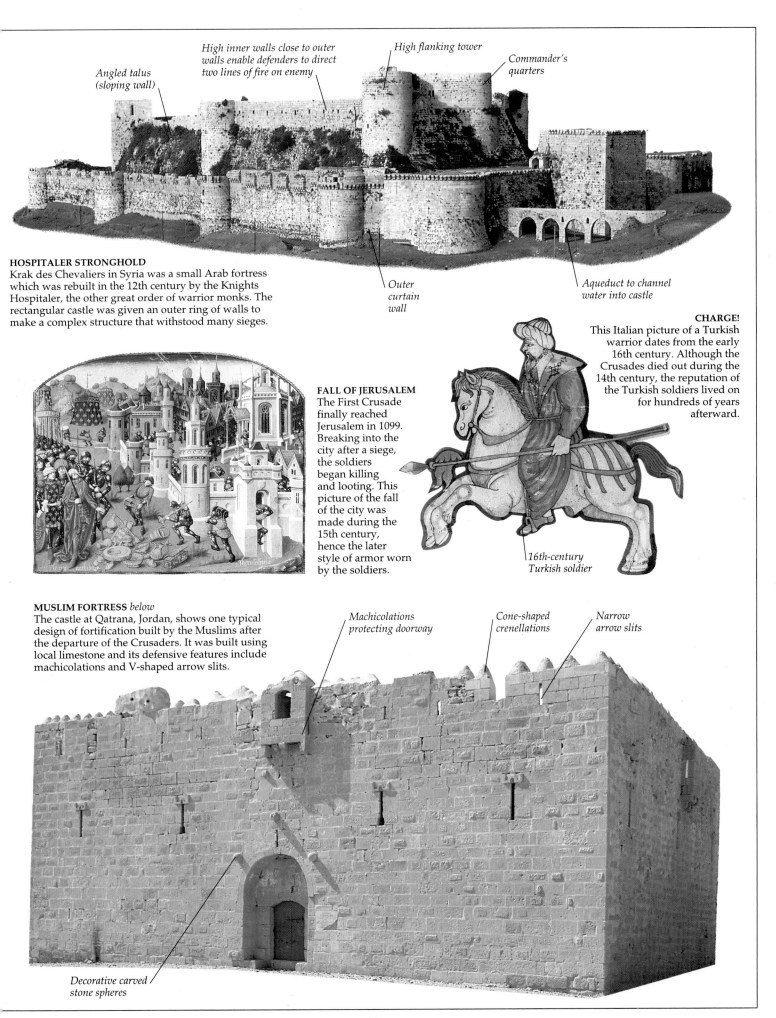

HOSPITALER STRONGHOLD
Krak des Chevaliers in Syria was a small Arab fortress which was rebuilt in the 12th century by the Knights Hospitaler, the other great order of warrior monks. The rectangular castle was given an outer ring of walls to make a complex structure that withstood many sieges.

Angled talus (sloping wall)

High inner walls close to outer walls enable defenders to direct two lines of fire on enemy

High flanking tower

Commander's quarters

Outer curtain wall

Aqueduct to channel water into castle

FALL OF JERUSALEM
The First Crusade finally reached Jerusalem in 1099. Breaking into the city after a siege, the soldiers began killing and looting. This picture of the fall of the city was made during the 15th century, hence the later style of armor worn by the soldiers.

CHARGE!
This Italian picture of a Turkish warrior dates from the early 16th century. Although the Crusades died out during the 14th century, the reputation of the Turkish soldiers lived on for hundreds of years afterward.

16th-century Turkish soldier

MUSLIM FORTRESS *below*
The castle at Qatrana, Jordan, shows one typical design of fortification built by the Muslims after the departure of the Crusaders. It was built using local limestone and its defensive features include machicolations and V-shaped arrow slits.

Machicolations protecting doorway

Cone-shaped crenellations

Narrow arrow slits

Decorative carved stone spheres

Castles in Japan

FORTRESSES HAD BEEN BUILT in Japan since the Yamato period (A.D. 300–710). Sometimes these were temporary strongholds, but by the 14th century more permanent fortifications of wood were beginning to appear. The 16th and early 17th centuries, a time when castles were in decline in Europe, saw the heyday of castles in Japan. The reasons for this were the political instability in Japan and the use of small firearms. Cannons were not highly developed there, so warriors could shelter behind castle walls, safe against the handguns and cavalry of their enemies. Natural hill sites were used if possible; otherwise platforms of rammed earth were built and faced with smooth stone blocks. Rivers, lakes, or the sea provided natural moats.

MANY BAILEYS
Castles often contained many courtyards, which kept the main tower a safe distance from attempts to set it on fire. Progress through the courtyards was sometimes like going through a maze. An attacker would have to go through all the baileys before getting to the main tower.

NEW MONEY
Ieyasu was first of the Tokugawa shoguns, imperial officials who became the most powerful men in Japan. He reorganized Japan's monetary system in the late 16th century, using cast or beaten slabs of gold or silver for coins.

Silver coin, 1601

Gold coin, 1601

SWORD POLISHING
Polishers work on lethally sharp samurai weapons. In the later 16th century, samurai warriors often lived in large castles, as the daimyos (provincial rulers) began to replace their many small fortresses with single huge castles, often built in towns. Such castles became administrative centers as well as fortresses.

SAMURAI
The samurai was in many ways similar to the feudal knight of Europe. He was a trained warrior who served a lord and expected to be served by peasants and merchants. His armor was made in a unique way. It consisted of iron plates laced together. Because of the damp climate the iron was lacquered to keep it from rusting. This armor was effective against the very sharp swords that were the mark of the samurai. This picture shows a samurai warrior crossing the Uji River in 1184.

ATTACKING THE GATE
The assault on the Sanjo palace (1160) shows a common method of attack. This was rarely successful, unlike starvation or betrayal. Sometimes the garrison shot the attackers in the courtyard. Siege techniques were similar to those used in Europe, although mines were not used until the later 16th century.

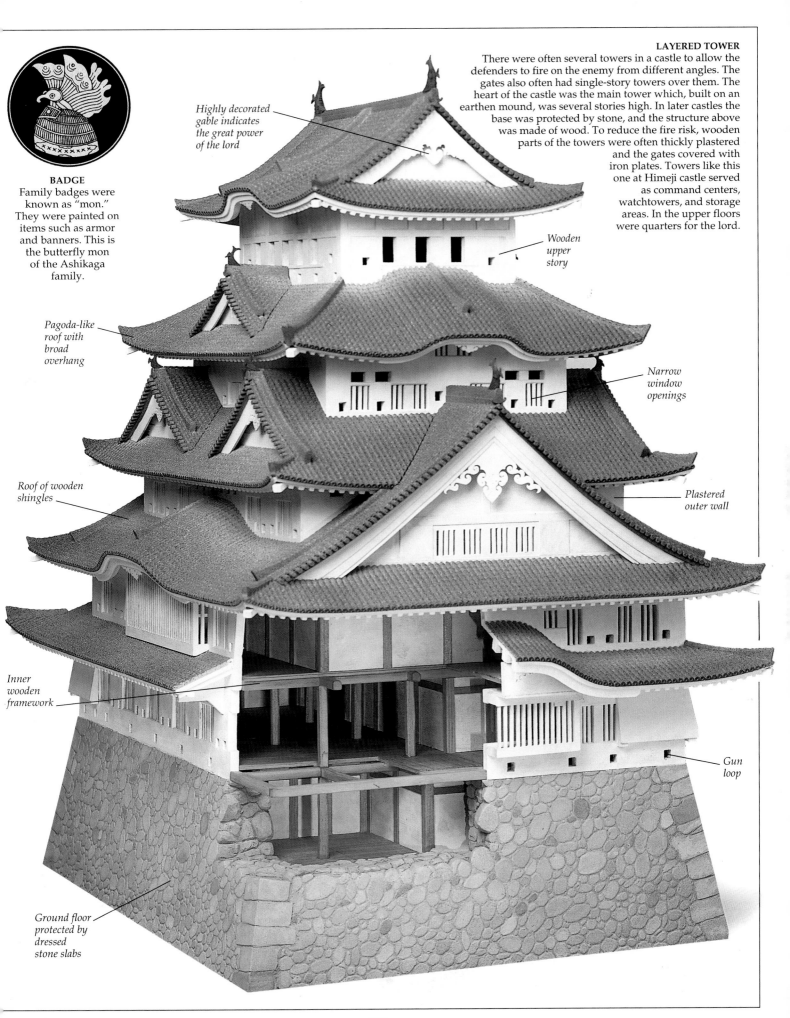

BADGE
Family badges were known as "mon." They were painted on items such as armor and banners. This is the butterfly mon of the Ashikaga family.

Highly decorated gable indicates the great power of the lord

LAYERED TOWER
There were often several towers in a castle to allow the defenders to fire on the enemy from different angles. The gates also often had single-story towers over them. The heart of the castle was the main tower which, built on an earthen mound, was several stories high. In later castles the base was protected by stone, and the structure above was made of wood. To reduce the fire risk, wooden parts of the towers were often thickly plastered and the gates covered with iron plates. Towers like this one at Himeji castle served as command centers, watchtowers, and storage areas. In the upper floors were quarters for the lord.

Wooden upper story

Pagoda-like roof with broad overhang

Narrow window openings

Roof of wooden shingles

Plastered outer wall

Inner wooden framework

Gun loop

Ground floor protected by dressed stone slabs

The great hall

THE HALL WAS the main room in the castle. It was used for eating, sleeping, and carrying out business. The day in the hall began early with breakfast, which consisted of bread soaked in ale or watered wine, eaten after Mass. The main meal, where formality and good manners were expected, was taken at about ten or eleven in the morning. In the evening there were various suppers, which often ended in overeating and drunkenness. Servants with pitcher, basin, and napkin poured water over the hands of important guests before and after meals; other people washed at basins near the doors. Later the trestles (table supports) were removed to make room for entertainment and eventually palliasses (straw mattresses) for sleeping. Only rich people had beds. In the 13th century the lord began to distance himself from the larger household; extra rooms were built for him and his close family.

12th-century copper-alloy hanging lamp

Holder for candle

Modern drip-catcher

HEARTH AND HOME
Early halls had a fireplace in the middle of the room but these were later abandoned in favor of wall fireplaces, which had the advantage of a flue to carry away the smoke. The lord's table was often near the fire for warmth; it was usually situated at one end so the lord could survey the hall. Often on a raised platform, the lord's table might be the only one with fixed legs and a tablecloth.

FLOORED!
A 13th-century tile illustrates the legend of Tristan. The floors of royal palaces, rich halls, and abbeys were decorated with many tiles like this. Carpets were sometimes imported as luxuries from the East, but they were usually hung on the walls, like tapestries.

Silver bird holds shield with heraldic arms of the count of Flanders

Gilded mount

Maple-wood cover

Bowl made from very finely cut maple wood

Animal decoration

Decorative enameled design

CANDLESTICK
Animals and plants decorate this late 12th-century copper-alloy German candlestick. Candles were made from animal fats. Oil lamps were also used.

YOUR HEALTH!
Covered wooden bowls were sometimes used for drinking toasts. They were called mazers, an old word for maple, the wood used to make the bowls. This 15th-century Flemish bowl has a gilded silver foot. It probably belonged to Louis de Male, Count of Flanders. Another precious vessel in the great hall was the salt cellar. This was placed in front of the principal guest at mealtimes; smaller "salts" were placed on other tables. Lesser folk sat "below the salt."

ROYAL HALL
Steps from the hall at Loches, France, led out to the battlements, marked by the round tower. Often the curtain wall formed one side of the hall. This saved money on building but meant that no large windows could be set into this side of the hall. Early halls had been made of timber, but stone became increasingly common. Because of the smell and risk of fire, the lord usually built his hall well away from the kitchen.

FORMAL MEALS
These took place in the great hall. Sometimes there was a lesser hall where the castle constable conducted business.

STEEP ROOF
The castle at Loches on the Loire River in France has a keep of the 11th and 12th centuries with many later additions. The royal hall with its stepped gable is associated with the 15th-century king Charles VII, whose mistress Agnes Sorel lived at Loches and is buried there.

Battlements of great hall

Conical, slate-covered roof

Door to tower and outer courtyard

Circular tower overlooks battlements, to give a good view of the surrounding area

Large upper windows of great hall

The kitchen

HOOKING OUT THE FOOD
A 14th-century cook uses a skimmer and a flesh-hook to handle pieces of meat.

IN THE MIDDLE AGES, the heat for cooking was provided by fires. Accidental fires could be disastrous, so the castle kitchen was often housed in a separate building in the courtyard. But this meant that the food cooled as it was carried to the table. So it became more common for the kitchen to be joined to the castle hall by a passage. It might contain an open hearth or ovens set into the walls. In addition there could be a range of other rooms nearby – a pantry (for storing food), a buttery (for bottles), a bakehouse, and perhaps even a brewhouse with a tank to soak barley and kilns to dry the grain.

Socket to take handle

SKIMMER
Many foods were cooked by boiling them in water. A tool like this skimmer could be used to remove small items from a cauldron. The hot water would drain away through the holes. There was originally a long wooden handle to prevent the cook's fingers from getting burned.

Holes through which water could drain

Hollow tube removes core, leaving the more edible parts

CORE OF THE PROBLEM
This object is probably an apple corer. It could be pushed into the middle of the apple to remove the core.

Wooden handle

LEGS TO STAND ON
Cooking pots with legs could stand right in the fire. The long handle helped to prevent burned fingers.

KNIFE
As today, knives of all sizes were used in the kitchen for cutting, carving, and boning.

FLESH-HOOK
This was a tool with metal prongs that were sometimes bent into hooks. Using the wooden handle, the flesh-hook could be thrust into a piece of meat to lift it into or out of a cauldron of boiling water. This was a common way of cooking meat.

Hooked prong

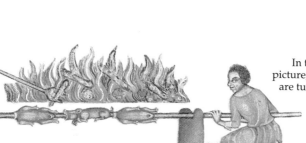

ON THE SPIT
In this 14th-century picture, several animals are turned on a spit so that they roast evenly. The man on the left puts a log on the fire using a long forked stick.

CLEAVER
The cook would cut up animal carcasses with a cleaver. It had a large, deep blade, because it was brought down through the meat like an ax. The weight of the blade, as well as its sharp, curved edge, helped to cut through the flesh.

SUGAR LOAVES
White sugar was a costly rarity in Europe – it had to be brought from the East. The lowest quality of refined sugar was the conical loaf shown here, which was made from white paste. Powdered white sugar, sometimes flavored with spices or flowers, was a luxury. There was also brown sugar and molasses, which came from Sicily.

Chains to hang pot

Carrying handle

Early 15th-century hairstyle

HANG IT
This flat-bottomed pot was hung over the fire, probably from a hook in the top of the fireplace.

Decorative animal-head spout

FASHIONABLE POT
By the 13th century, pots made of iron, bronze, or copper were gradually replacing those made from earthenware. Round-bottomed ones, like this bronze cauldron, or kettle, were designed to be hung from chains over a fire. This one has been decorated with moldings of animal faces, and each attachment for the hanging chain is shaped like a woman's face. The hairstyles help date the pot as early 15th century.

Spout in shape of animal's face

JUG
Many jugs were made of pottery, often with the green glaze typical of medieval ware. In order to make them more attractive, potters sometimes molded faces or animals into the surface. Here there is a decorative spout shaped like an animal's head.

Broad, heavy blade

At the table

A VARIETY OF FOODS was served in the castle hall. Beef and mutton (sheep) were the main meat dishes, but venison (deer) was eaten after a successful hunt. Because there was no refrigeration, animals were kept near the kitchen until ready for slaughtering. Otherwise meat was salted to preserve it. Rich sauces were used to disguise the taste of over-ripe meat. Poultry and eggs were often eaten, wild birds of all kinds ended up on the menu, and game was popular. The meat might be eaten with onions, garlic, and herbs from the castle garden, and the most common vegetables were dried peas and beans. Fish was served on Wednesday, Friday, and Saturday, and also during Lent. Salted herrings were common, but the castle fishponds provided freshwater species too. At feasts or royal meals, more exotic items, such as peacock or crane, were served. The most spectacular dish was the chef's dish "subtlety," a mixture of sugar, paste, marzipan, and jelly, painted and molded into shapes like castles or ships.

Pheasant tail feather replaced after cooking

Plain, earthenware finish

WHAT A DISH!
Some animals were made to look alive for presentation at the table, for example by replacing feathers. Medieval people often liked their food to be artificially colored with fruit or vegetable juices.

Handle

DRINK, ANYONE?
Crude pottery jugs were used to carry ale or wine for the ordinary diners. Hops were unknown until the later Middle Ages, so beer was made from barley, wheat, oats, or a mixture of all three. Women known as ale wives, or monks in monasteries, did the brewing.

FRUITFUL FARE
Castles often had walled gardens with orchards where fruit like this could be grown. Apples and pears grew in northern latitudes; farther south grew figs, grapes, oranges, and lemons.

Pewter plate

Pewter bowl with decorated edge

BOWL

This 12th-century bronze bowl is called a Hansa bowl. The Hansa was a league of North European trading towns, where these bowls were widely used. Metal bowls were cleaned after use by boiling them in bran and then rubbing vigorously with a soft cloth.

Lid shaped like human face

HERE'S LOOKING AT YOU

The lid of this copper-alloy jug has been made with a face staring up, and the legs have feet shaped like animal paws. A jug like this might have contained hippocras, a drink made from wine mixed with honey and herbs.

Animal foot

BANQUET

Nobles were often served by pages who were training to become squires. In this 15th-century picture most people sit on benches – only the rich used chairs. People had personal knives and spoons (pp. 48-49), but forks were almost unknown. Often, two diners would share a bowl or even a cup.

PUDDING

This is an almond milk pudding. Milk was used mainly for cooking rather than drinking, and puddings like this were considered delicacies. One was custard: a pastry case called a coffin, filled with a mix of meat, herbs, dates, ginger, vinegar, and eggs.

Rose petal

BREAD PLATES

Flat pieces of stale bread, called trenchers, were used as plates. They soaked up the gravy and, if uneaten afterward, could be given to the poor or thrown to the dogs. Whole wheat bread was the most common. Wastel was the finest white bread, eaten by the rich. Grain for the bread came from local manors and the bread was baked in the castle kitchen or bakehouse.

The entertainers

LIFE IN A CASTLE was not all work and warfare. Hunting and hawking were greatly enjoyed by all and brought useful additions for meals. Some outdoor pastimes were quite dangerous – there were tournaments for the knights, and bouts of wrestling or rough ball games. Adults even played children's games such as blindman's bluff, during which a person's head was covered and he or she had to chase the other players. To while away the hours indoors, people played board games and listened to musicians or storytellers. The storytellers recited the great heroic epics of champions such as Roland, troubadours in southern France sang of their love for ladies, and chivalric romances, such as tales of King Arthur's knights, were also popular. Much of this entertainment was provided by traveling minstrels and players, who moved around, but some kings and nobles kept a jester, or clown, to entertain them.

Hood to keep bird in the dark

Thick glove protects falconer from the bird's sharp talons

Leather jesses keep bird on the fist

GAMBLERS
Men often gambled at dice and became addicted to it.

ROYAL PLEASURE
This lead badge shows a king riding with his falcon. All ranks of society enjoyed falconry, although some species of bird were reserved for the nobility. Falconry was a skill that had to be learned, but great pleasure was taken in working birds with a decoy bird (or lure) and watching their soaring flight and their ability to plummet down through the air to seize their prey.

BIRD IN THE HAND
People often had close relationships with their falcons. A lord might keep a falcon in his chamber, although they were usually kept in special buildings called mews. Some of the equipment used in falconry, such as the hood, came to Europe from the Middle East at the time of the crusades.

HAWK BELLS
Bells were attached to the bird's leg so that the falconer knew where the creature was.

GARDENER'S WORLD
Castle gardens were usually well tended, not least because they grew herbs and fruit for the table. They were also pleasant places for lords and ladies to stroll and talk.

BEATING TIME

The merrier medieval tunes had a strong drum beat, which sometimes had a complex pattern. These small drums, in a picture from the mid-14th-century Luttrell Psalter (Psalms), are called nakers. A very large drum was sometimes carried on the back while someone else struck it.

MINSTREL

A 15th-century musician plays a hornpipe, so-called because its wooden pipe is connected by a leather band to a hollowed-out cow's horn. Dancing to the accompaniment of musicians playing instruments like this was very popular. The earliest forms involved everyone holding hands in a ring or a long chain. Later there were more dances for couples. Minstrels also sang, sometimes accompanied only by the harp. Early songs often dealt with war; later, love songs and songs with a religious theme became popular. There were some songs that reminded people how Jerusalem was ruled by Muslims and urged Christian crusades to win it back.

Wooden pipe

Slashed sleeves

Leather band

Checkered pattern often worn by entertainers

Hollowed-out cow's horn

Woollen tights

HURDY-GURDY

A 14th-century musician is playing a hurdy-gurdy. This was played by turning a handle which sounded all the strings at once to produce a drone-like sound. The fingers of the other hand were then used to produce the required notes.

WHAT A FOOL

The job of the fool or jester was to make people laugh. He might wear a cap and bells and carry a bladder on a stick (the slapstick), and his jokes could be very crude. He was sometimes allowed to say things to his master that others dared not.

BALL GAMES

This 15th-century ball game with curved sticks may be an early version of hockey. The ball used was quite large and was probably made of leather.

Women and children

THE MOST IMPORTANT woman in the castle was the lady, the wife of the lord. The families of knights might also live in the castle, and the children of other lords might be trained there. High-ranking women had their own ladies-in-waiting to attend them, and there were also female servants. Laundresses cleaned soiled clothes and seamstresses repaired them. Women of all classes learned how to spin, weave, and sew, and some ladies of rank were skilled at embroidering in gold and silver threads.

SIDE SADDLE
The Wife of Bath, from Geoffrey Chaucer's late 14th-century *Canterbury Tales,* had been married several times and showed that women sometimes had a degree of independence.

HIGH AND LOW
This 15th-century picture of a well-dressed lady and a female laborer shows the differences in the classes of society. As in many pictures of the time, the peasant is shown digging, with her back bent.

HEAD OF STONE
This 14th-century stone corbel, carved to represent a woman, once jutted from a wall to take the weight of an arch or beam. The woman wears a wimple, a piece of linen which passed under the chin. The wimple was popular throughout the Middle Ages and was often worn with a veil. Married women often covered their hair as a mark of their position and age.

Wimple, fastened to the hair by pins

Veil

PLAYING AT SOLDIERS
This little metal toy sword and helmet are copies of full-size items used in war. Young boys, who might one day use real arms in battle, probably played with these.

Sword

Helmet

Children

When only about seven, a boy from a noble family might be sent to a castle, often that of a relative, to become a page and learn good manners. After about seven years he would begin to train as a squire, perhaps being knighted when about 21. Girls were also sent to another castle to be taught by the lady in the arts of sewing, homemaking, and how to behave correctly – especially in front of the gentlemen.

BRINGING UP BABY
Childbirth was often dangerous, for medical knowledge in the Middle Ages was limited and standards of hygiene were low. Many mothers and babies died, but families were still often large. Noblewomen sometimes gave their babies to wet-nurses to breast-feed rather than doing this themselves.

TOGETHERNESS

Knights and nobles often married an heiress for her land. In spite of this inauspicious start, couples often grew close. People of lower rank had a wider choice of partner, although anyone serving a lord usually had to get his permission to marry.

Amethyst

English cross-brooch

Sapphire   *Ruby*

Late 13th-century English gilt brooch

THE LADY

This lady of the early 15th century would run the household in her husband's absence and check his nearby manors. She also had to entertain visitors to the castle, greeting them at the gate and being there to say farewell. She was in charge of the castle kitchens and the menu, although she would not normally cook the food herself. In her spare time she would enjoy hunting, dancing, and playing chess and other board games.

SIGNS OF WEALTH

Ladies wore costly jewelry – because it looked attractive, because of its fine workmanship, and because it showed how rich they were.

Padded roll over net

Plackart

Kirtle

Leather strap

HARD SOLE

Pattens were shoes with raised wooden soles. They could be slipped over ordinary leather shoes if the weather was bad. They were useful when rain made tracks and roads very muddy.

Solid wooden sole

Tight-fitting sleeve

Sideless surcoat

CHRISTINE DE PISAN

This well-educated woman wrote poems and other works in the late 14th century and became a professional writer in the early 15th century.

Train

The lord

A CASTLE WAS HOME TO A LORD, who could be anyone from a minor baron to the king himself. A large castle could be used as an administrative base by a powerful lord, who could also live there in comfort. The lord's rank meant that he enjoyed the luxury of privacy, with his own chamber. Kings and great lords, who had several castles and houses, would appoint an official called a castellan to run the castle in their absence. But if during a siege the castellan felt it necessary to surrender, the laws of war said that he should first send word to his lord for permission to do so. The king would also entrust some of his castles to local officials such as sheriffs, who could govern part of the country using the castle as a base. Such castles were usually built in towns and would often be connected to the town walls.

KING'S COIN
This gold coin is a bulla, made for Edmund, King of Sicily.

Dogs like greyhounds were valued hunting companions

HOMECOMING
A 14th-century knight returns home. He is wearing a large steel helmet called a basinet. A lookout watches from his lofty perch in a high tower.

PERSONAL ITEMS
A lord would usually have his own cutlery, which might be kept in a leather case. These are two of a set of four knives which are decorated with the heraldic arms of John the Fearless, duke of Burgundy.

HAT TRICK
This lord wears a chaperon, a distinctive 15th-century hat. It developed from the hood. The long "tail," originally the back of the hood, is called a liripipe.

KEEPING FIT
The lord was a knight and was expected to fight for his king if necessary. Many practiced by taking part in tournaments, where mounted knights fought in front of admiring ladies. Knights could enter either the team game (the tourney) or single combat with lances (the joust). In this 15th-century picture, two knights have shattered their lances against one another and are fighting with swords.

Carving knife

Eating knife

Enameled arms, used between 1371 and 1404

IVORY CASKET
Caskets contained personal possessions and came in various sizes. This French example is made from ivory and is carved with scenes from the Romance of the Chateleine de Vergy. It was made in the second quarter of the 14th century.

ON DISPLAY
Lords displayed their wealth
not only on themselves but also
on their family and retainers.
This early 15th-century buckle,
found at Chalcis in Greece,
is made of silver.

THE LORD
Men who looked after small castles,
particularly in the unsettled period between
the 10th and 12th centuries, were not always
too fussy about their dress. But those in
charge of larger castles were often keen to
impress others with the richness of their
clothes, especially on formal occasions such
as feasts or a royal visit. This 15th-century
lord wears a long formal gown called
a houppelande.

*Collar of
linen shirt*

*Collar with
badge*

*Pendant
with badge*

*Gilt decoration
covering
silver metal*

Linen shirt

Bagpipe sleeves

*Belt carrying
purse*

Velvet gown

Silver

Woolen hose

UNDERWEAR
In the 14th and 15th centuries
a man would wear a shirt beneath
his outer garments. In contrast to the
other clothes, the shirt was plain and
functional. Because it was worn next
to the skin it was made of linen, to
prevent itching. On their legs men
wore warm woolen hose.

*Pointed
leather
shoes*

SHOWING OFF
This early 14th-century
decoration made from
gilt silver was worn on
a belt. Like the buckle
at the top of this page,
it was found at
Chalcis in Greece.

49

Fabrics and textiles

IN THE MEDIEVAL PERIOD people usually made their own clothes, either spinning and weaving the cloth themselves, or buying linen in large amounts and making up garments when needed. Wool was the most common textile and was often woven with goat's hair to make chamlet, an ideal material for making clothes. The wealthy might wear garments of more expensive cloths, such as linen or silk. Everyone wore underclothes of linen, because they were comfortable next to the skin. Many varieties of silk became available during the Middle Ages, including samite, damask (from Damascus), and taffeta.

DYING FOR A LIVING
Cloth could be colored by soaking it in a tub filled with a natural dye. Such dyes were usually made by boiling the roots or leaves of certain plants in water. Buttermilk (the liquid fat left after making butter) was a useful whitener.

Wooden distaff

Thread

Fleece

Whorl

Ball of wool thread

WORKING WITH WOOL
Once sheared from the sheep and washed, the fleece was carded – stroked with a toothed tool to untangle it and make the strands point in one direction. These strands were then wound around a distaff and fingerfuls of wool were pulled away and twisted into a single thread.

Blade

Cloth shears

Sharp inner edge

Shearing shears

Springy rounded end

CUT A DASH
Wool was sheared from the sheep using large shears. Smaller versions would be used to cut the cloth. Unlike scissors, which have two arms that pivot at the center, the arms of shears are joined at one end and they cut when the two arms are pressed together so that the blades slide over each other. The rounded end of the shears is springy, and the blades open automatically when released.

Steel blade

Distaff

Leatherworking

Shoes, saddles, clothing, scabbards, belts, and straps for pieces of armor were just some of the items made from leather. Molded leather was even used to make pieces of armor, as an alternative to steel. It was also used to make jugs and buckets. Many leather objects were skillfully decorated with cuts, holes, or molded designs.

AT WORK
This 15th-century picture shows leatherworkers at their trade.

SHARP BLADE
This knife was used for cutting through hide. The leatherworker moved the handle back and forth so that the whole blade sliced through the leather. Leatherworkers still use similar tools today.

Pushing this large
wheel around makes
the distaff turn

Drive thread
connects distaff
with large wheel

Worker's hand
pulls fleece out
into a thread

Fleece

SPINNING A YARN
Most girls and women were taught
to spin. This 14th-century woman is
using a spindle wheel. With this device,
a push of the large wheel keeps the distaff
turning, so that the yarn winds onto it as it is
pulled out into a thread. This technique could be used to produce
different grades of yarn. Coarse wool, such as blachet, was used
for items like bed covers. The coarsest types, russets and burels,
were used mostly by the poor. Wool yarn was woven into cloth on a
loom. Knitting began in the 15th century and in some places only
became a craft a century later.

51

In the fields

THE PEOPLE WHO LIVED and worked in a castle had to eat, and horses and hunting dogs had to be fed. Much of the food was grown in the surrounding fields, which belonged to the lord of the castle. The workers who tilled these fields lived in villages nearby. In times of trouble they and their animals could seek shelter within the castle walls. Producing food was hard work in the Middle Ages. It meant getting up very early in all weather at all times of the year, in order to plow the fields, sow the seed, and harvest the crops in autumn. In sunny areas grapevines were grown to produce wine. Beer brewed from barley was popular in northern Europe; the water was so dirty that drinking it could make people very ill.

SOWING
Seed was carried in a bag or pouch and scattered over the earth by hand. Birds often managed to take some of the seed for themselves.

PRUNING
In March the vines were pruned with a short-handled billhook, which could cut the branches back to ensure good growth.

PLOWING
The iron plowshare turned over a furrow in the earth ready for planting crops. Usually the plow was pulled by oxen. Eight animals were sometimes used, but generally it was four or less, as shown on this 14th-century tile. The peasants joined forces to provide enough animals to pull the plow.

SICKLE
The sickle was used to cut crops in July; the stalks were left half-cut to provide straw for cattle. The wheat or barley would then be threshed to separate out the grain, which the miller ground down to make flour for bread-making.

Ears and grains of emmer wheat

Iron sickle

WINNOWING
This miniature, from the early 15th-century *Très riches heures* of the Duke of Berry in France, shows the month of June. It is represented by men using scythes to cut the hay and two women tossing up the hay to winnow it. The hay provided winter fodder (animal feed) for the cattle.

HEAVE!
This 14th-century haycart is being pushed uphill. Solid collars on the horses enabled them to pull without choking.

SON OF THE SOIL

A peasant was not usually allowed to leave the land his family worked. He was a serf or villein, which for some was little different from being a slave, except that medieval peasants had to feed themselves from what they grew. The lord took a percentage of the crops for himself and the peasant had to grind grain in the lord's mill, for a price. A peasant's life was often very hard. He was dependent on the weather, and ruined crops meant famine. The Black Death killed many peasants in the 14th century and they became more valued by the upper classes as a result of this.

Leather cap

WINE

The vines are being carefully tended in this 15th-century Flemish picture. Once ripe, the grapes were picked and packed in large casks where barefoot workers trod them to squash out their juice. The juice was collected and left to ferment until it formed wine.

HARD WORK

This 15th-century illustration from the Book of Hours of the Duchess of Burgundy shows the task for March: hoeing the ground to break up the topsoil for planting.

Tine

Coarse woolen tunic

PITCHING IN

The pitchfork had two prongs, called tines, and a long wooden shaft. It was used mainly for thrusting into sheaves, or bundles, of hay and pitching them up on to a wagon.

Leather bag

Ax head

AX

A multipurpose tool, the ax could be used for felling small trees, for chopping up firewood, or for cutting logs.

"Beak"

Warm woolen hose

BILLHOOK

This tool was used for pruning. It had a long cutting edge and a "beak."

Tough leather boots for hard work

Animals in the castle

A CASTLE NEEDED ANIMALS to provide food for the occupants. Some animals could be kept in the courtyard; others grazed in the fields and were brought in at night or at times of danger. Many of the animals would be killed as winter came – there would not be enough fodder to feed them all until the spring. The carcasses would be salted or smoked to preserve them and hung in storerooms. Medieval farm animals looked different from those of today. Medieval animals were smaller and gave less meat, milk, or wool than their modern counterparts. But some of the old breeds have survived, or have been "bred back," and show what these animals were like. To add variety to the table, wild animals were hunted as extra food.

COTSWOLD SHEEP
Medieval sheep were smaller and thinner than sheep today and their meat would probably have been less tender to eat. But they were very useful animals. Their skins were used to make parchment for writing on and their wool was vital for clothing. In the 15th century, English owners made fortunes by selling wool to make cloth.

SWEETENERS
Sugar was rare and expensive, so honey was often used as a sweetener. These beekeepers use wicker hives.

Hive (or bee-skep) made of wicker

MONTH BY MONTH
This 12th-century ivory counter is part of a game set. Each one shows familiar country scenes that portray two months of the year.

Zodiac sign of Aries the ram, representing April

January represented by a man carrying sticks

Long, curved horns

BAGOT GOAT
Goats provided milk and were unfussy eaters in the castle courtyard. Bagot goats probably arrived in Europe in the 14th century, brought by crusaders returning from the Holy Land. Their name comes from Sir John Bagot, to whose park they were presented. In 1380 a goat's head was added to the Bagot family's coat of arms.

FRESH EGGS
Chickens could be left to scratch around inside the castle courtyard. They might be tied to a post to keep them from wandering.

PORKER
Medieval pigs were much more like wild boars in shape and were nowhere near as fat as modern pigs. In medieval England they were not only useful for providing pork, they were sometimes trained as retrievers, like modern dogs, and were used when hunting.

Dark, hairy skin, like that of a wild boar

CONEY
Rabbits were caught for food, and for their fur, which was called coney. A ferret was put down a rabbit's hole and the rabbit was caught in a net as it bolted out the other end.

Rabbit warrens, or burrows, were specially set up, and looked after by an official who was called a warrener.

PHEASANT
The Romans probably introduced pheasants to England. People hunted them with bows and arrows or falcons to provide a source of additional food.

PANNAGE
To overcome winter food shortages, pigs could be driven into the local woodland in November. Here, as this 15th-century picture shows, people knocked down acorns from oak trees for the pigs to eat. The pigs also liked beechnuts. The right to pasture pigs in a forest was known as pannage.

Attractive brindled coat

Wide horn span – horns were left uncut in the Middle Ages

Long, shaggy hair keeps goat warm in winter

Udder – cattle were a source of milk as well as meat

LONGHORN
Unlike the cattle of today, whose horns are removed for safety, medieval cattle could have very long horns indeed. Longhorn cattle may be descended from the wild cattle first domesticated in the Stone Age. Cattle provided meat, and their hides were tanned to make leather. The steers were harnessed to a plow with a wooden yoke (horses were not often used for this task). The cows were milked, as were ewes and she-goats.

The castle builders

Oɴᴄᴇ ᴀ sᴜɪᴛᴀʙʟᴇ sɪᴛᴇ with fresh water was found, the lord employed a master mason, often on contract, to help plan and build the castle. Such highly respected men would employ a clerk to sort out the accounts and obtain building materials. The master mason would take charge of the building work. Under him were an army of workers. Hewers cut the stone at the quarry; freemasons cut the fine blocks of building stone (known as ashlar) and carved decorative moldings; roughmasons and layers built the walls. There were many other workers doing specific jobs, from carpenters to well-diggers, metalsmiths to quarrymen.

STONE ME
A 13th-century mason wearing a cloth coif on his head shapes stone blocks while a basket of stone is sent up to the workman waiting at the top of the building.

CROWBAR
Heavy blocks of stone needed to be manhandled from quarry to building site and into their final position.

CHISELING IT OUT
From the 12th century on, chisels were used more and more, replacing axes for stonecutting. Masons used a mallet and chisel to carve decorative designs into stone.

DIVIDERS
By setting a distance between the two arms, dividers could be "walked" across a piece of stone to fix a measurement. They could also be used like a compass, to make circles or curves.

MEN AT WORK
Workers supply stone blocks using a wooden ramp and a type of wheelbarrow. Often rough stone-and-mortar walls were faced with ashlar. If the whole wall was not faced, ashlar would be put around doors, windows, and loopholes.

MORTAR TROWEL
Mortar was mixed and laid on with a trowel. The mortar was made by mixing sand and lime; the latter could be provided by burning limestone on site. Mortar bound together the rubble walls of rough stone and the fine ashlar facings. It was also used to build the brick castles which appeared in the later Middle Ages.

SHAPING UP
Shaping stones was skilled work. A 15th-century mason inspects a fine squared stone block to ensure it will fit.

Measuring arm

MASON'S CHISEL
Chisels were used for cutting and dressing stone, although some stone was soft enough to be cut with a saw. A smith was needed on site because the tools wore out quickly.

VAULT
In order to carry the weight of a stone roof, builders of the Norman period used a tunnel effect called a barrel vault. By crossing two of these at right angles a groined vault was made. Here we see the outer part of the vault as it rises upwards from a corner.

Groin

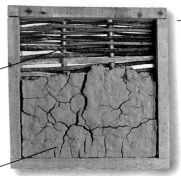

Wattle (interwoven branches)

Daub, a mixture of straw, mud, and manure

STRAIGHT MAN
A lord talks with his master mason, who carries a plumb line. The lead weight on the end keeps the line hanging straight down, so one can check verticals.

Plumb line

COUCY-LE-CHATEAU
This is a model of the great tower of Coucy-le-Château at Aisne in France. It was built between 1225 and 1245 by Duke Enguerrand III. The tower was very strong, with great arches intersecting in the middle. Even if an enemy broke into one of the niches, the wall arch around it would prevent the stonework from collapsing.

Parapet to protect soldiers on gallery

WATTLE AND DAUB
Many of the buildings in a castle courtyard might be framed with wood. The gaps between the wooden uprights were often filled with panels of interwoven branches, called wattle, plastered with daub.

Gallery

Passageway within thick outer walls of great tower

Window with stepped opening

Fireplace with chimney built into wall

Entrance to great tower

Stone arched bridge to castle entrance

PULLEY
A 13th-century mason uses a pulley to haul up a basket full of stone.

Moat

The woodworkers

WOODEN CASTLES were far more common than those of stone before the 12th century. Professional woodworkers were needed to cut the timber for palisade fences and walkways, the gate tower, motte tower, bailey buildings, and sometimes facings (called revetments) covering the slope of the motte and the bailey ditch banks. When stone castles became popular, some of the defenses were still made of wood. In addition, large amounts of wooden scaffolding were needed as the building rose up. Courtyard buildings were often made of wood or built with a wooden frame. Even in stone buildings wood was used for roof and ceiling beams and floors. Inside, carpenters made doors, shutters, partitions, paneling, and furniture. During a siege they would make catapults and other machines (see pp. 24–25) to help defend the castle.

HOARDINGS
Removable wooden hoardings were supported on beams pushed into holes called putlog holes below the battlements.

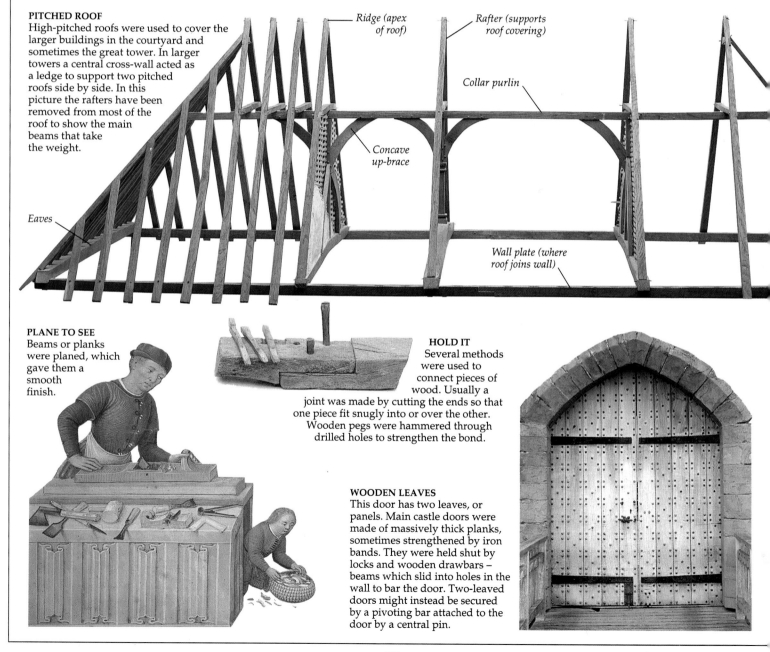

PITCHED ROOF
High-pitched roofs were used to cover the larger buildings in the courtyard and sometimes the great tower. In larger towers a central cross-wall acted as a ledge to support two pitched roofs side by side. In this picture the rafters have been removed from most of the roof to show the main beams that take the weight.

Ridge (apex of roof)

Rafter (supports roof covering)

Collar purlin

Concave up-brace

Eaves

Wall plate (where roof joins wall)

PLANE TO SEE
Beams or planks were planed, which gave them a smooth finish.

HOLD IT
Several methods were used to connect pieces of wood. Usually a joint was made by cutting the ends so that one piece fit snugly into or over the other. Wooden pegs were hammered through drilled holes to strengthen the bond.

WOODEN LEAVES
This door has two leaves, or panels. Main castle doors were made of massively thick planks, sometimes strengthened by iron bands. They were held shut by locks and wooden drawbars – beams which slid into holes in the wall to bar the door. Two-leaved doors might instead be secured by a pivoting bar attached to the door by a central pin.

BAD WORKER
This early 14th-century tile from Tring, England, shows a master craftsman telling off a worker for cutting a beam too short. Workers of various professions were organized into guilds, with rules and standards of quality to be kept up.

SAW POINT
These workmen are cutting a large piece of wood with a two-handed saw. Sometimes a saw-pit was used, the lower-ranking man standing in the pit, where he was showered with shavings.

Auger

Hammer

TOOLS OF THE TRADE
The tools used by medieval carpenters were very similar to those of today. The auger was twisted around to bore holes; the handsaw cut small pieces of wood. The metal parts were made by a smith (pp. 60–61).

Handsaw

CARPENTER
Skilled woodworkers were always in demand because of the large number of objects made from this material. Unlike today, large areas of countryside were covered in woodland and forest, and timber was carefully managed to make sure supplies were always at hand. Once a castle was built there was always need for a carpenter to repair or replace damaged items, or woodwork damaged by insects, fungi, or the damp.

Tie-beam

Awls

Billhook

Broad ax

Adze (for cutting slivers from the surface)

Chisel

Metalwork

CLOSE WORK
If a seamstress needed a thimble to protect her finger, a metalworker had to make it. This one might have been bought from a market, a shop, or a traveling merchant.

METALS OF ALL KINDS were used in castles. Iron was needed for a number of different everyday things, from horseshoes and harnesses to parts for siege machines, door hinges, tools, and hoops for barrels. Nails, both large and small, were used by the thousands for joining wood to construct palisades, wooden buildings, and parts of buildings such as roofs and doors. All these items had to be made by a metalworker (or smith) in the castle itself. The lord would frequently buy armor for himself and his knights from local merchants. A rich lord might even have some of his armor made abroad. But weapons and armor were in constant use. They were damaged in training and rivets would work loose. A castle armorer was needed for equipment repairs.

STRIKING A POSE
The smiths in this 15th-century manuscript are busily hammering metal into shape over a solid iron anvil, their tools hanging behind them. Some anvils had a "beak" at one end, which was used to shape metal objects like horseshoes, but the anvil used by armorers was often a simple cube of iron. Most smiths' workshops were housed in a separate building to reduce the risk of the rest of the castle catching fire.

ARMED AND DANGEROUS
Armor and weapons like those of this 16th-century knight were often damaged in battle or tournament. An armorer who could do repairs, replace loose or broken rivets, and make pieces of mail and plate armor when needed was a valuable asset in a castle.

Cutting edge

A SNIP
Snips were for cutting sheets of metal to give a basic shape to work on.

HOLD ON
Tongs were for holding metal when it was being hammered, especially when it was red hot.

Handles

Metal tools

These medieval tools are little different from those used today. Armorers had extra tools, such as a huge pair of snips, set vertically with one end fixed to a block, to cut sheets of steel for making plate armour.

NIPPERS
The pincers could cut through wire. They have a swiveling fastener to hold them closed.

Swivel fastener

COPPER
A 14th-century smith shapes copper. Softer than other metals, copper was used for decorative work.

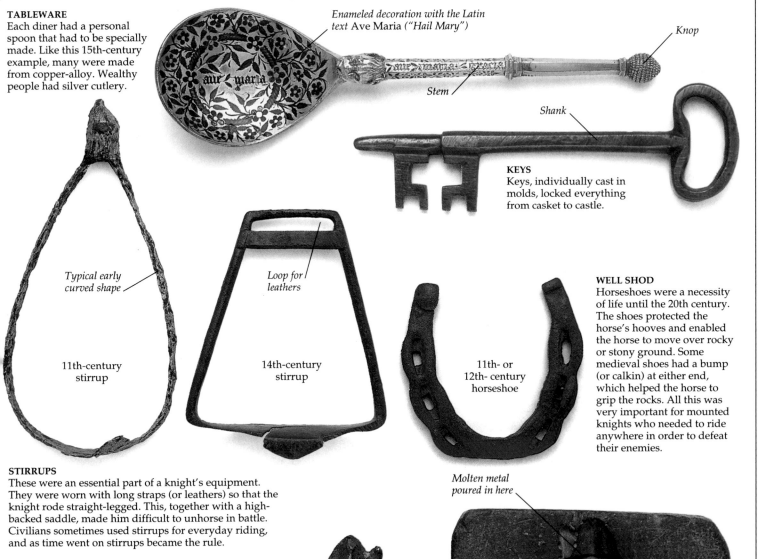

TABLEWARE
Each diner had a personal spoon that had to be specially made. Like this 15th-century example, many were made from copper-alloy. Wealthy people had silver cutlery.

Enameled decoration with the Latin text Ave Maria *("Hail Mary")*

Knop

Stem

Shank

KEYS
Keys, individually cast in molds, locked everything from casket to castle.

Typical early curved shape

11th-century stirrup

Loop for leathers

14th-century stirrup

11th- or 12th- century horseshoe

WELL SHOD
Horseshoes were a necessity of life until the 20th century. The shoes protected the horse's hooves and enabled the horse to move over rocky or stony ground. Some medieval shoes had a bump (or calkin) at either end, which helped the horse to grip the rocks. All this was very important for mounted knights who needed to ride anywhere in order to defeat their enemies.

STIRRUPS
These were an essential part of a knight's equipment. They were worn with long straps (or leathers) so that the knight rode straight-legged. This, together with a high-backed saddle, made him difficult to unhorse in battle. Civilians sometimes used stirrups for everyday riding, and as time went on stirrups became the rule.

Molten metal poured in here

FORGE
This 19th-century picture of a forge shows that metalworkers were still using similar tools and techniques as their medieval counterparts..

MOLDED
Some items were made by melting metal and pouring it into a mold. This 15th-century figure is made from lead, which melts at a low temperature and was therefore easy to cast in this way. Lead was often used for making badges.

Figure

Mold

Castles in decline

EXPLOSIVE PIONEER
Roger Bacon was a Franciscan monk who lived in England and France in the 13th century. He was particularly well known for his writings on science and technology and was the first Western writer to describe how to make gunpowder. His recipe appeared in a book published in 1242.

BY THE END OF THE 15TH CENTURY, castles were losing their military importance. Societies gradually became more stable, and people demanded more comfortable living conditions. Gunpowder appeared in Europe in the early 14th century but did not have any great effect on castles at first – they were still being built 200 years later. From the 16th century on, some castles continued in military use, especially in danger areas such as Austria, a buffer zone protecting western Europe from the Turks. Other castles were used as army barracks. Fortified tower-houses were still built in places such as Scotland and Ireland, where riots or raids by neighbors made protection necessary. But many castles fell into ruin; the stone was even stolen and used in buildings elsewhere. In the 18th and 19th centuries there was new interest in castles as symbols of the medieval world.

TURKS ATTACK
In 1453 the Turks managed to break into the heavily fortified city of Constantinople (now Istanbul), which was one of the last strongholds of the Christian Byzantine empire. The formidable walls were attacked by land and sea, and the Turks used numerous guns to make holes in the walls.

DEAL
The fort at Deal, England, was built by Henry VIII in the 1530s as part of a chain of similar defenses on the English coast. The low, rounded gun platforms deflect enemy missiles and present less of a target to cannons, but fortifications using arrowhead-shaped bastions were already taking over in Europe.

VASE GUN
The earliest pictures of cannons are English and appear in 1326. They show a vase-shaped object which would have been strapped down to a wooden stand. Such guns shot large metal darts and may have been aimed at doors to frighten defenders and keep them from coming out.

Wooden tiller

Removable breech-block containing powder charge

Iron straps to secure barrel

Muzzle

CANNON
Huge guns called bombards were developed to blast walls with enormous stone balls. Smaller cannons, like this replica, were also increasingly used. This one has ropes for carrying, but by the 15th century some cannons had wheels.

Ropes for carrying

FAIRY-TALE CASTLE
The German castle of Neuschwanstein was built by King Ludwig of Bavaria in the late 19th century. It is one of several 19th-century castles created by people who were influenced by a romantic image of the medieval world.

Notch in which to rest gun

Copy of late 14th-centry handgun

Wooden pavise, or portable shield

Heraldic badge to identify the lord of this marksman

Iron barrel

Steel kettle-hat

Coat of plates, a garment lined with steel plates riveted inside

Steel buckler, or fist-shield

Wooden prop

Steel spike to stop shield slipping

HANDGUNNER
Early handguns were fired either by a hot wire pressed against the touch-hole, or by a glowing slow match made from cord soaked in saltpeter (potassium nitrate). Some guns had a lug on the bottom to hook over walls and absorb recoil. Inside a castle, guns could be fired through round loopholes in the walls or long horizontal slots for larger weapons, which would be fired at a besieger's cannons or earthworks. Later, guns were often arranged in groups, and this technique led to the building of forts that could hold batteries of guns. Unlike medieval castles, these forts were usually built and run by the state.

Index

Acknowledgments

Dorling Kindersley would like to thank:
The authorities of the following castles and museums for permission to photograph: Caerphilly castle, Dover castle, Hedingham castle, Château de Loches, Marksburg, Pfalzgrafenstein, Château de Saumur, British Museum, Museum of London; Alex Summers and the Order of the Black Prince for providing models and objects for photography; the Cotswold Farm Park for providing animals for photography; Gordon Models for model-making; Joanna Cameron for illustrations; the following people for acting as models: Penny Britchfield; Dorian Davies, Paul Elliott, Robin Pritchard; Nicki Sandford for costumes; Caroline Giles for hair and make-up; Plantagenet Somerset Fry for consultancy.

Picture credits
a=above, b=below, c=center, l=left, r=right, t=top
Aerofilms: 6bl, 9tl
Ancient Art & Architecture Collection: 6cl, 12tl, 32bl, 33tc, 34cr
Bridgeman Art Library/British Library: 7rc, 15bl, 22tr, 24tl, 33tr, 39tl, 40tl, 40bl, 43lc, 44tr, 44br, 45tl, 46tl, 47bl, 50tc, 52tl, 55tl, 57tl; /Ecole des Beaux-Arts, Paris: 58bl; Bibliothèque Nationale, Paris: 24bl, 35lc, 53tl, 56lc; /University of Oxford for the Bodleian Library: 29cl, 45lc, 48c, 54lc; /Musée Conde, Chantilly: 45br; /Giraudon/Musée Conde, Chantilly:

52tr; /Bibliothèque Municipale de Lyon: 25tr; Laros-Giraudon/Bibliothèque Municipale, Rouen: 50bl; /By Courtesy of the Board of Trustees of the Victoria & Alberrt Museum: 15tc; /Victoria & Albert Museum, London: 52rc
British Museum: 22cl, 38cl
Britstock-IFA: 6tr
Bulloz/Ecole des Beaux-Arts, Paris: 59tc
Jean-Loup Charmet: 20bl
E.T. Archive: 20tl, 25cl, 27br, 30cr, 31tl, 31bc, 41tl, 48lc, 55tr, 60tr, 60br, 62cl, 62tr
Mary Evans Picture Library: 18 cr
Werner Forman Archive/Museum of Catalan Art, Barcelona: 17tl; /Boston Museum of Fine Arts: 37br; /Burke Collection, New York: 36tl; /Kita-In, Saitumu: 36c
Robert Harding Picture Library: 8cl, 10lc, 11tc, 28b, 28tl, 29tl, 35t; /British Library: 42tl; /British Museum: 10tr;

Bibliothèque Nationale, Paris: 26tl, 47tl
Michael Holford: 8tr, 16-17, 16tl, 36bl
His Grace the Archibishop of Canterbury and the Trustees of Lambeth Palace Library: 32br
Mark MacLoskey: 6-7
Mansell Collection: 62tl
National Portrait Gallery, London: 32cr
Syndication International: 17tr; /Biblioteca Medicea Laurenziana, Florence: 43tr; /British Museum: 22tl, 52br, 56bc; /Musée du Petit Palais, Paris: 46br; /Trinity College Dublin: 57br
ZEFA: 17cr, 18tr, 20-21, 63tr

Every effort has been made to trace the copyright holders and we apologize in advance for any unintentional omissions. We would be pleased to insert the appropriate acknowledgement in any subsequent edition of this publication.